STILL CONNECTED

W9-AWO-679

STILL CONNECTED

FAMILY AND FRIENDS IN AMERICA SINCE 1970

CLAUDE S. FISCHER

Russell Sage Foundation • New York

Library of Congress Cataloging-in-Publication Data

Fischer, Claude S., 1948–
  Still connected : family and friends in America since 1970 / Claude S. Fischer.
    p. cm.
  Includes bibliographical references and index.
  ISBN 978-0-87154-332-5 (alk. paper)
1. Interpersonal relations—United States. 2. Social networks—United States.
3. Families—United States. 4. Friendship—United States. 5. Social isolation—United States. 6. Social interaction—United States. 7. Communities—United States. I. Title.
  HM1106.F55 2011
  302.30973'09045—dc22

2010033277

Text design by Suzanne Nichols.

RUSSELL SAGE FOUNDATION
112 East 64th Street, New York, New York 10065
10 9 8 7 6 5 4 3 2 1

In memory of
Harold H. Kelley,
mentor

Contents

About the Author

Claude S. Fischer is professor of sociology at the University of California, Berkeley.

Preface

IN 1970 PAUL MCCARTNEY sued to dissolve the Beatles. Also in 1970, the ABC television network tried a novel experiment: showing football games on Monday night. (In 1970 the game, a movie on NBC, and a sitcom on CBS were the three national television choices available to American viewers.) In 1970 math students carried slide rules to do their calculations. (Those under age fifty-five or so can look up "slide rule" in Wikipedia.) A year or two later, the first portable calculator, the Sharp EL-8, would appear and sell for about $2,000 in 2010 currency; it could do little more than add, subtract, multiply, and divide. And in 1970, if Americans wanted to be "in touch" with their family or friends, they had three choices: traveling, writing a letter, or making a telephone call from a home, office, or public booth. Calling Los Angeles from New York cost about a dollar a minute in today's currency.[1] In 2010 things would be quite different (although Paul McCartney would still be around).

This short book seeks to answer one basic question: Did Americans' social bonds with family and friends change between the 1970s and 2000s, and if so, how?

In the 1970s, I would have referred to Americans' "social networks," but one development since then has been a change in the meaning of "social network." In the 1970s, a relatively small and somewhat isolated group of social scientists (including myself) used the term to mean the set of relationships among individuals, organizations, or groups—as in "the network of medical research labs" or "the network of Chicago art dealers." We had to explain the phrase to laypeople, pointing out, for example, that we did not mean a television network such as ABC. Then the term spread and was transformed into "networking," as in using contacts and pull to get a job. Most recently, "social networking" has come to mean Internet services that facilitate online communication, such as MySpace and Facebook. From 1851 through 1980, the phrase "social network" appeared only seventeen times in the *New York Times;* its frequency doubled during the 1980s, doubled again in the 1990s, and then increased more than tenfold in the 2000s.[2] The word "networks" had become popular, but its meaning had changed. This book is about neither "networking" nor far-flung "social networks," but about Americans' relationships to the people with whom they are close—basically to family and friends.

What has happened to such relationships since 1970? I look for the answer in various surveys done over the last forty years and am thus captive to the questions that survey researchers asked over those years. The answer is, as a result, tentative. Nonetheless, it appears that Americans' relationships with family and friends were—perhaps surprisingly to some commentators—robust and lasting.

Acknowledgments

THIS BOOK was made possible by a sabbatical from the University of California–Berkeley and a visiting scholar appointment at the Russell Sage Foundation in New York City in 2009–2010. I thank director Eric Wanner and the RSF board for their invitation—and Eric also for the book title. I warmly thank the Foundation staff for the quick and plentiful support they provided, including computer help, library research, and clerical work. My fellow scholars at the Foundation (including my wife, Ann Swidler) provided daily sparks of inspiration. It was a great place to work.

Peter Marsden's detailed reading of the initial draft and comments by Alexandra Marin improved the book, but they, of course, are not accountable for remaining errors. Cynthia Buck's editing did wonders for the prose. April Rondeau shepherded the book through production, and Suzanne Nichols expertly managed the whole affair.

CLAUDE S. FISCHER
BERKELEY, CALIFORNIA
SEPTEMBER 2010

Chapter 1

Alone in America?
The Issues at Stake

IN MID-2006, a story on findings from a survey spread through the media: "Study: 25% of Americans Have No One to Confide In," announced *USA Today* on June 23. "Americans Have Fewer Friends, Researchers Say," reported ABC News on the same day. National Public Radio headlined "Social Isolation: Americans Have Fewer Close Confidantes" on June 24. The *Boston Globe* took two bites at the story: "It's Lonely Out There" on June 23 and a column by Ellen Goodman on June 30, "Friendless in America." "Nearly a Quarter of American Adults Have No Close Friends, Survey Finds," added Reuters on June 27. Last, but now making it officially a fact, the *New York Times* declared on July 2, 2006, that "The Lonely American Just Got a Bit Lonelier."[1]

These stories—and many more—reported the conclusions of an article published that year in the *American Sociological Review*. Miller McPherson and his colleagues Lynn Smith-Lovin and Matthew Brashears compared data from the 2004 General Social Survey (GSS) to those from the 1985 GSS. (The GSS is a repeated survey that has collected representative data on the American population about every other year since 1972.) The authors focused on a question the GSS asked in both 1985 and 2004: "From time to time, most people discuss important matters with other people. Looking back over the last six months, who are the people with whom you discussed matters important to you?" The finding that stirred such notice was that the percentage of respondents who said that they had discussed important matters with *no one* tripled—from about 8 percent to about 25 percent from 1985 to 2004—and the average number of names that respondents gave dropped from about three to about two. "Friendless in America" indeed.[2] It later turned out, although the media ignored it, that this finding was controversial. I argued in a 2009 publication that the results were anomalous, that the dramatic difference between the two surveys was probably due to changes in procedures, a technical problem, or perhaps both.[3] By the time this book appears, a GSS

1

experiment conducted in the 2010 survey should have shed some light on what happened in the 2004 survey.

Whatever the outcome of that study, the breathless coverage of the first report demonstrates readers' interest—mirrored by journalists—in personal relationships. The stories tapped Americans' long-term fascination with and concern about "community," a concern evident in the reception of books such as Robert Putnam's *Bowling Alone* (2000), *Habits of the Heart* by Robert Bellah and his colleagues (1985), and, going back sixty years, David Riesman's *The Lonely Crowd* (1950). Academics' interest in this topic burgeoned in the last few decades, and the number of social science articles focusing on "social networks" grew rapidly.[4]

For some scholars, social networks are theoretically important because they describe the framework of society: underneath the wallboard, plaster, and paint of social values and cultural practices is the timber skeleton of interconnections. Society *is* a network linking nodes, and people are nodes in the network. Other scholars are interested in social networks because they describe the personal environment of individuals and provide a way of mapping the social worlds in which they operate. With that tool, researchers can understand how individuals are supported, stressed, and generally shaped by their social milieus and, reciprocally, how individuals select their associates and structure their social milieus.

Policymakers, too, have found the network concept useful. For example, in the early 1980s the California State Department of Mental Health tried to capitalize on research showing that having close family and friends seems to bolster health. It mounted a campaign encouraging Californians to develop friendships, because "Friends Are Good Medicine"—the slogan appeared on bumper stickers and shopping bags—and could, officials thought, replace state health spending.[5] More recently, experts have turned to social network analysis as a tool for, among other things, tracking terrorists and tracking teenagers who spread AIDS.[6] The focus of this book, however, is more prosaic: we will be looking at changes in Americans' connections to family and friends between 1970 and 2010. Did Americans have more or less contact with kin? Did they gain or lose friends? Did they find more or less support from their close ties? Did they find more or less intimacy?

Changes in the Personal Ties of Americans

Periodically, the media find a piece of social science research that seems to reinforce the prevailing cultural theme that social bonds are fraying away, leaving individuals cut off and alone. In the 1970s, the journalist Vance Packard's best-selling book *A Nation of Strangers* warned that

Americans had become so mobile and so rootless that they were losing personal connections and becoming alienated and subject to all sorts of ills—even though, in fact, rates of residential mobility had been steadily *declining* for at least two decades. In the 1970s and the 1980s, too, "loneliness" was a topic of concern. The *New York Times* health editor, Jane Brody, wrote in 1983:

> Loneliness is now a national epidemic, according to many sociologists and psychologists, who point to such contributing causes as our highly techno-logical society where many workers interact more with machines than with other people; to our mobility, with the average American moving 14 times during a lifetime; to the impersonality of large urban settings where many people don't even know their immediate neighbors; to the prevalence of divorce, which now ends half of American marriages.[7]

In the late 1990s, Robert Putnam's work, culminating in his 2000 book *Bowling Alone*, garnered tremendous coverage for reporting that between the 1950s and the 1990s Americans became much less civically active. Although Putnam's findings were focused on political and organiza-tional participation, the changes he reported were mostly of modest size, and his analysis was nuanced, the message that reviewers and readers took home was that community ties were (still) shriveling. The final example, from the 2000s, is the report on "Social Isolation in America" by McPherson and his colleagues in which they record stark declines in Americans' lists of confidants. (Oddly, in all four cases, my own initial response was "Not so fast."[8] Twice is a coincidence, three times a habit, and four times must signal an obsession.)

Understanding what happened to Americans' personal networks is not only a matter of curiosity. There are broader intellectual claims at stake here. Has, for example, "post-industrial" or "postmodern" life, with its supposed cultural fragmentation and myriad distractions, frayed Americans' social ties?[9] Or has the turn of the millennium instead enabled individuals to choose from a wider array of people and groups and thus enriched their social lives?[10] Or has an expansion of social choices only confused and discouraged Americans?[11]

And there are pragmatic concerns at stake too. Despite the overhyp-ing of California's "Friends Are Good Medicine" campaign, our physi-cal and psychological health are in some ways bolstered by the practical and emotional support of our family and friends.[12] To be sure, the very same people can also undermine our health.[13] (In the social world from which I came, illnesses were often explained as the consequence of "aggravation"; aggravation, in turn, was caused by refractory children.) Still, it is usually better to be socially engaged than not.

The answer also matters for, we might say, the national psyche. Americans seem discouraged about the general state of relationships. They tend to believe, for example, that American family life is in decline. (Note, however, that Americans exempt *their own* families from this sad judgment. It is *other Americans'* families and friendships that are fraying.[14]) It would be perhaps valuable to national morale to have an accurate sense of what has happened to Americans' social bonds.

Obviously, this topic fits into the vast discussion around the "decline of community." I will not address that subject explicitly here—I have done so elsewhere[15]—because that controversy is about long-term changes, perhaps starting when gentlemen wore powdered wigs, and it is about a broader set of issues, including civic life, politics, and national culture. This book has a more modest agenda. Specifically, it asks whether relationships with family and friends changed between 1970 and 2010 in terms of how many kin and friends Americans had, how often they saw or communicated with family and friends, the extent to which they received practical or emotional support from family and friends, and how they felt about their relationships.

Sources of Possible Change

Why might Americans' personal ties have changed significantly? There are many ideas about the forces that may have been at play, ideas that usually predict a deterioration of personal relationships. For the most part, this book does not test explanations, mainly because the available data make it very hard to do so. For example, it is difficult to distinguish whether a change in how often young adults see their parents is the result of new forms of communications or the result of Americans marrying later; both trends developed rapidly between 1970 and 2010. This book focuses on just getting a sense of the forty-year changes in social ties themselves. Still, it is important to at least outline the new circumstances that might have altered Americans' personal relationships. There are many, gathered here into four categories.

Technological Changes

The most visible development of the last forty years has been technological innovation. Modern cars and planes, email, cell phones, text messaging, video links, and social networking sites vastly expanded, sped up, and lowered the cost of social interaction. To technological enthusiasts, this meant that individuals' relationships multiplied and deepened as they revived high school friendships, saw grandchildren a continent away babbling on a computer screen, joined online "communities" of people with shared interests or problems, and acquired

hundreds of Facebook or MySpace "friends." To technological pes-
simists, this multiplication of virtual ties only dissipated and demeaned
authentic human relationships. For example, the literary critic William
Deresiewicz wrote in 2009:

> Friendship is devolving, in other words, from a relationship to a feeling—
> from something people share to something each of us hugs privately to
> ourselves in the loneliness of our electronic caves, rearranging the tokens
> of connection like a lonely child playing with dolls. . . .
>   The more people we know, the lonelier we get. . . .
>   We have given our hearts to machines, and now we are turning into
> machines. The face of friendship in the new century.[16]

Absent definitive data, how much difference these technologies
have made to personal relationships we will probably never know.
But the media are rife with speculations about the new technologies' consequences for personal relationships and personality. For example, in
2009 the *New York Times* reported that the Internet provided elderly people with life-invigorating social connectivity. "I was dying of boredom,"
said one elderly woman, but online social networking "gave me a reason
to keep on going." An expert on aging told the reporter: "The new future
of old age is about staying in society, staying in the workplace and staying very connected. . . . And technology is going to be a very big part of
that, because the new reality is, increasingly, a virtual reality. It provides
a way to make new connections, new friends and new senses of purpose."[17] The same year, however, the *Times* published an article on the toll
that frequent text messaging was taking on teenagers; texting, according
to one psychotherapist, "offers companionship and the promise of connectedness. At the same time, texting can make a youngster feel fright-
ened and overly exposed."[18] What is the poor *New York Times* reader to
believe?

Adoption of the new e-communications, then, may have profoundly
altered Americans' relationships. In chapter 6, I briefly review the research
on the new technologies and connect its findings to the trends displayed
in this book.

Demographic Changes

Americans consider marriage and parenthood as key steps in attaining
adulthood.[19] In 1970 the median American man married (for the first
time) at age twenty-three and the median woman at age twenty-one; in
2009 the ages were twenty-eight and twenty-six, respectively.[20] Five more
years of bachelorhood and spinsterhood had been added to the typical
life cycle. (If we treat cohabitation as a sort of marriage, the change is not

as great, but unions of cohabiting couples in this period were not as stable as those of married ones.[21]) In the mid-1970s, about 30 percent of American women age twenty-five to twenty-nine had yet to be mothers; in the mid-2000s, about 45 percent of women of that age had yet to be mothers. So, about 2 million more twenty-something women were childless in the 2000s compared to the 1970s.[22] Note that the total American birthrate changed little after 1973; the timing of births, however, moved forward.[23]

So, in the 2000s more young Americans had yet to "settle down." Many of them, especially those from the middle class, were spending their "emerging adulthood"[24]—the time between age eighteen and attaining the job-and-family markers of full adulthood—getting more education and training for careers. Many in the working class were awaiting stable employment. Young adults were also spending much of that time avoiding commitments to institutions, such as work, politics, or church, and devoting a great deal of energy to their churning personal relationships.[25] This demographic development should have affected Americans' overall ties to friends and families.

Three other demographic trends also deserve mention: immigration, aging, and residential rearrangement. One trend is the huge flow into the United States of immigrants, particularly from Mexico and Asia. Bringing with them their own social customs, recent immigrants focus their lives around family and fellow immigrants and, perhaps most important for our purposes, are partially cut off by language and culture from the great majority of Americans. Many of these newcomers do not appear in the national surveys we rely on because interviews are usually done only in English. Therefore, their effects on the trends we can measure are underestimated. In 2006 and 2008, however, the GSS did interview many respondents in Spanish. These interviewees reported considerably less social activity than did the English-language interviewees, even those interviewees who were Hispanic.[26] To the extent that immigrants affected the social life of the English-speakers living around them, they probably reduced the average volume of social activities a bit.

A second demographic trend is the changing "population pyramid"— that is, the distribution of Americans by age—created by changing birth and death rates. As I noted, American birthrates changed little after 1970, but they had dropped considerably in the decade before, reducing the proportion of young people in the population. Also, from 1970 into the 2000s, the life spans of Americans, especially of American men over age sixty-five, grew by a few years.[27] Thus, the overall American population aged. And older people tend to have fewer social connections. (Some observers might claim, however, that sixty-five is the new fifty-five.) Birth and death rates also affected how many relatives Americans had—a point I return to in chapter 3.

The third demographic trend after the 1970s is the continuing shift in where Americans live: fewer live in rural areas, and more live in suburbs—although the scale of this rearrangement is not close to what Americans experienced earlier in the twentieth century. Based on what we know about place and relationships, the post-1970 residential redistribution might have nudged the average American involvement with kin and neighbors down a bit and raised the average involvement with friends up a bit.[28]

None of these three demographic influences was probably as consequential as emerging adulthood, but all need to be considered in interpreting trends in social connections.

Economic Changes

The early 1970s are notable in part because they marked a significant turning point in American economic history. It was the end of the postwar economic boom and of the large-scale government activism that had vaulted a large chunk of the population into the middle class—the middle class of families with a salary-earning husband and his homemaker wife who were financially secure, suburban, home-owning parents of college-bound children. And it was the beginning of a now-longer period of negligible economic advancement for most Americans marked by stagnating wages for men and, partly as a result, increasing employment for married women. The proportion of married women age twenty-five to sixty-four who worked rose from about one in three in 1960 to about two in five in 1970—still a minority—and then to about seven in ten in the mid-1990s and beyond.[29] Where employed wives had been an exception, they were now the norm. Cultural shifts (discussed in the next section) helped motivate this march out of the kitchen, but feeling financially strained also moved women to seek paid work. The massive shift of so many wives and especially mothers of young children from the home to the workplace should have set into motion many changes in their relationships—and those of their husbands—such as, perhaps, turning their attention from neighbors to coworkers.[30]

Over the same period, more Americans worked nonstandard hours—nights, weekends, odd combinations of hours—as the U.S. economy moved toward a 24/7 schedule. Although some of that shift-shifting provided flexibility that workers could use to ease work-family tensions, much of it was involuntary. And in any case, odd hours put people literally out of sync with many of their family and friends.[31]

Shrunken or stagnating incomes and wealth—or at least, the sense of financial constraint—probably also affected relationships. Financially comfortable people can afford to travel more, go out more, entertain more, stay in touch more, and thus expand their networks more than those who are financially strained. Alternatively, well-off people can forgo borrowing from or entertaining friends and family because they have the money to buy it all in the marketplace—they can hire a moving company rather than ask friends to help them move, or spend a weekend in Atlantic City or Las Vegas rather than endure a house visit with the in-laws. Empirically, wealthier people have more social relationships—specifically, more nonkin relationships—than less affluent people. To the extent that average Americans lost ground economically—or at least felt that was happening[32]—the change might have narrowed their circle of friends.

Cultural Changes

Cultural shifts independent of economics, demography, or technology may also have altered Americans' ties to family and friends. The leading candidate for such a consequential shift is the changing role of women. Along with joining the workplace, women have redefined the terms of most American institutions, marriage and family most of all, grasping more independence and more power. Much of the movement toward gender equality occurred before 1970, but it accelerated in the years afterwards.

Other cultural influences are perhaps too glacial and long-lasting to have made much change in the 1970 to 2010 window. One is the development in the West of what Abram de Swaan called "widening circles of identification"—increasing sympathy for ever-more-distant people, such as AIDS victims in Africa.[33] Similarly, some historians describe a long-term change in Americans' emotional makeup, including the development, especially among the nineteenth-century bourgeois, of greater emotional sensitivity and self-control.[34] Even vaguer are the frequent references to the "zeitgeist" of a historical period—the 1960s were years of counterculture and free love, the 1980s were years of greed, and so forth—or the "ethos" of a generation: the generation that grew up in the 1930s and 1940s is industrious and family-oriented, the 1960s generation is alienated and individualistic, and their children, the "Me Generation," are self-absorbed and hypersocial.

It is difficult to study cultural shifts of this sort empirically. Often, they appear as the residue of explanations: changes that cannot be explained by economics, demography, technology, or historical events scholars then attribute to a vague cultural force. And yet, as hard as it is to pin down such effects precisely, there is something about "climates of opinion" that sociologists find real.

These four categories do not exhaust the possible explanations for changes in social relationships that we may observe. Political events and their consequences, for example, might shape personal life by arousing popular disillusionment, through scandal and war, with civic life. But these four categories cover much of the speculation and permit us to think about the broader social changes that could have affected personal ties and how they did so.

Resilience

For all the societal changes in America since 1970, it may turn out that people's ties to family and friends were robust and that social connections survived, kept their shape, and kept their functions—in other words, that not much changed. Perhaps a few of the developments I just reviewed counterbalanced one another. For example, maybe new communications technologies offset tighter family budgets to leave Americans with about the same means to pursue social connections. Maybe having more mothers in the workforce reduced Americans' involvement with neighbors but expanded their involvement, to about the same degree, with coworkers. More profoundly, these technological, demographic, economic, and cultural developments, however significant they appear, may have been insufficient to significantly disrupt people's ties to family and friends because those ties are especially important to people and are therefore especially *resilient* to change.

As people encounter new circumstances—new devices, economic restructuring, social fashions, and so forth—they adapt in ways that sustain their key relationships. "Adapt" has two different English meanings. As a transitive verb, people adapt something "to make [it] suitable . . . for a specific use"; as an intransitive verb, people adapt to a circumstance.[35] We can presume that people place their close friendships and, especially, their immediate families very high among their priorities (see chapter 3). People thus try to adapt their environment, notably new technologies, to the purpose of sustaining those relationships. That may mean, for example, using new media to remix the combination of calls, letters, and visits with family and friends so as to sustain about the same level of total involvement as before, at the level each individual prefers.

Intransitively, people adapt themselves and their habits when they cannot change the environment. A key example is how American mothers dealt with a new economy, new norms for women's roles, and higher expectations for children (see chapter 3). Prioritizing their children, they made other adjustments in less critical or at least more malleable activities—notably, doing less housework, sleeping less, entertaining less, and spending less time with their spouses. Some things must change in people's lives when external conditions change sharply, but people protect their core relationships. As one review of the social consequences of the Internet concluded, "Some of the most important parts of life [close ties] . . . are comparatively stable . . . and resist change."[36]

Lower on the priority list, and thus more vulnerable to fluctuation, would be the more peripheral relationships that people have—the "weak ties" with "consequential strangers."[37] There is the growth, for example, of Facebook-type "friends." Very occasionally, one of these people enters a person's inner social circle, but for the most part social networking ties are casual associations. (Social networking scholar danah boyd has reminded blog readers that Facebook-type "networks" differ considerably from "personal networks." For example, your mother may be in the latter but not the former.[38]) This is the region of people's social worlds where we would expect major expansion and contraction as even minor changes in circumstances occur. Say, if the cost of computing or emails goes down or up, the volume of acquaintanceships might sharply balloon or shrink in response, while the number of close ties stays the same.

To be sure, family and friendship bonds *do* change under radically new conditions. There is evidence, for example, that Chinese relationships changed significantly when a market economy rose to replace the Maoist command economy; evidence also shows that the privatization of Russian agriculture in the 1990s led to new patterns of social ties among villagers.[39] I know of no hard data on how other major events—say, the division of India in 1947, the Rwandan genocide, or, for that matter, America's Great Depression—altered personal relationships, but I assume that there were important social consequences. Indeed, people in stormy seas probably hold on even more tightly to immediate family and friends. Societal changes can significantly alter personal relationships, but people value family and friends highly, and they presumably try to adapt circumstances and adapt themselves as much as necessary to preserve those "resilient" ties.

Strikingly, while the question of whether and how Americans' close bonds changed in recent years is a subject of much talk, it is the subject of little systematic research.[40] The major exception is Robert Putnam's landmark work, *Bowling Alone,* to which this study certainly owes a great deal.[41] I do not address the central topic of Putnam's book—Americans' participation in formal organizations and political activities—but much of what follows here builds on and extends chapter 6 of *Bowling Alone,* entitled "Informal Social Connections." This book expands the range of data and pushes forward the time frame—and it comes to somewhat different conclusions.

Chapter 2

Studying Personal Networks

In 2004, Peter Bearman and Paolo Parigi published an article provocatively entitled "Cloning Headless Frogs and Other Important Matters." The authors reported some findings from a survey in which they had posed a question used by many scholars to study social networks (including the scholars who in 2006 reported a great jump in isolation; see chapter 1). They had asked North Carolinians what they were thinking of when they answered the question, "Over the last six months . . . have you discussed important matters with anyone?" Besides discovering that respondents had very diverse notions of what "important matters" were (one mentioned the cloning of headless frogs), they found that half of those respondents who had answered "no"—they had not discussed important matters with anyone—went on to explain that they had had nothing at all important to discuss in the prior six months.[1] Perhaps they just wanted the poll-taker to get off the phone. This account, and others like it, do *not* show that this question is useless, but it illustrates the point that any single measurement of people's social connections is bound to be partial, confounded, and idiosyncratic.[2] This chapter is about the issues and techniques of measuring people's ties to family and friends.

If we are to compare the characteristics of Americans' relationships over time, we must ask a set of procedural questions: What do we mean by "relationships to family and friends" or, more generally, by "personal network"? What sorts of things can we systematically observe that reflect these networks with reliability and validity? What distortions are introduced by each of the observational procedures? Ideally, we would resolve these questions a priori were we embarking on original data collection. This study, however, summarizes many different, completed data sets with varying procedures and measures. We must accommodate that variability and triangulate toward consistent findings.

Those readers who are interested only in the findings can skip ahead to chapter 3. Those who are especially interested in the measurement and methods issues should consult the notes for this chapter for extensions of various points.

A Definition of "Personal Network"

A personal network can be defined as the set of people from whom a person receives and to whom a person gives goods, services, information, or emotion—and the relationships among all those people.[3] More concretely, it consists of the people with whom we live, hang out, work, talk, and trade; the people whom we help and who help us; the people from whom we get love and to whom we give deference; the people who we know care about us, as well as the people who give us trouble; and the nature of the bonds among those people.[4]

This definition requires several comments. Abstract as it is, it covers a wide range of people in the life of the average American today—probably in the high hundreds or more, according to network analysts' estimations (even *excluding* Facebook or MySpace "friends").[5] It includes everyone from spouses to the office mail delivery person with the latest watercooler gossip. Obviously, for most purposes, a researcher limits his or her canvass of social ties to the subset of especially "important" people, perhaps limiting the study to those who are emotionally involved with the individual or arbitrarily keeping the list down to, say, the individual's "three closest friends." This book largely focuses on individuals' immediate, personal networks—usually up to about two dozen people with whom they are most deeply involved—although at some points we have to use whatever implicit definitions of the network the survey researchers used.

Ideally and occasionally, researchers know something about the bonds among the "alters"—the individuals on the other ends of the person's social bonds. Are the respondents' close friends, for example, also close friends with each other? I focus here on the set of people with whom individuals are *directly* involved. This decision is not meant to slight the importance of "friends of friends" or connections of "six degrees."[6] People are affected by those who are two or three steps away, although the degree to which they are affected is a matter of debate.[7] The focus of this book, however, is on the immediate set of personal ties—the ones about which the popular and scholarly concern around community is focused—and in any case, there are precious little representative, overtime data on friends of friends.

The definition I provided is stated in the present tense, but if we count only the people with whom an individual is involved at one moment, or perhaps even in one year, we would miss latent yet potent relationships. There is, for example, the old college roommate who could be expected to put you up if you visit Seattle, or the rarely seen aunt back home who would spring into action if your elderly mother needed assistance.

Researchers must decide whether and how to include such inactive but potentially critical ties. Many researchers expect to find important but latent relationships by asking respondents about scenarios such as: "If you were sick in bed for a couple of weeks, who do you think would help take care of you?"

The definition I provided highlights *positive* interactions, but most ties of any significance involve both positive and negative elements. Grandparents, for instance, may provide babysitting services to their adult children—accompanied by critical remarks about how the grandchild is being raised. People also occasionally have relationships that are mostly negative—for example, with annoying coworkers. For all the talk of personal networks as sources of "social support"—as in the California "Friends Are Good Medicine" campaign (chapter 1)—relationships are also the prime sources of tribulation.[8] Thus, personal networks provide social support, but are not the same thing as social support.

The definition stipulates that *exchanges*—help, companionship, advice, and so forth—constitute relationships. Scholars commonly describe, if only implicitly, the substance of relationships in two other ways. One of these alternative approaches sees relationships as formed by culturally determined *roles:* people are connected to their children, neighbors, coworkers, and so forth. The other approach sees relationships as constructed by *sentiment:* people are connected, for example, to those to whom they "feel close." These three options—defining personal networks by exchange, by role, or by sentiment—can yield somewhat different pictures of personal networks. For example, some people have relatives— siblings perhaps—with whom they rarely exchange a thing. Some people are highly involved with individuals who have no clearly specified "role" in their lives; vaguely defined "friends" fall into this category. And some important relationships, perhaps those with neighbors or coworkers, may be devoid of sentiment. This distinction—exchanges, roles, and sentiment—will arise again later when I discuss specific approaches to studying social ties.

For all these definitional niceties, this study, because it relies on existing data, must draw on research using a variety of (often implicit) definitions. In practice, fortunately, there is a lot of overlap in exchange, role, and sentiment when we look at people's immediate relatives and close friends.

Further Distinctions

Personal relationships differ from one another in many ways. Distinguishing kinship ties and nonkinship ties is critical. These bonds develop very differently: an individual is born into most kin ties and then later acquires other kin ties as a lagniappe of marriage. Both law and social norms treat kin ties as special and as different from friendship. (A recent law journal article, however, argues that the law *should* recognize the duties and rights of friendship.[9]) Kin have legal responsibilities for one another. Dropping a friend or acquaintance is common, but "dropping" a parent or child is shocking. Kin ties are far more likely than nonkin ties to connect people of different gender and disparate ages. If you are close to someone twenty-five years older or younger than yourself, that person is almost always a relative. Too often, researchers have ignored this simple distinction, pooled all ties together, and gotten puzzling results that should not have puzzled them.

There is also the distinction between the "core" and the "periphery" of the personal network. Having peripheral ties—casual friends and acquaintances—can still be consequential: these people—say, sorority sisters from your college years—can provide information, help, and further connections that your closer friends cannot. Having a dispersed network of acquaintances—coworkers from an old job perhaps, or the parents of a child's classmates—provides access to information and assistance that is not available from family and friends.[10] It is probably optimal, in the end, to sustain personal networks composed of many diverse acquaintances *and* intimate ties. In this book, I occasionally draw on descriptions of individuals' full networks—for example, a question asking respondents to estimate the number of people with whom they are in regular contact—but the focus here is on the more intimate circle.

Network scholars have elaborated many typologies and dimensions in addition to the kin-nonkin and core-periphery distinctions to describe specific relationships and full networks.[11] Yet the sparseness of trend data on Americans' ties from 1970 to 2010 makes these extra distinctions largely moot.

So far in this chapter I have focused on how a researcher might think about the study of people's ties to family and friends. How have they done so in practice?

Ways of Studying Personal Networks

Using the networks metaphor as a way of understanding individuals and society has developed relatively recently in the social sciences, although it has roots in classical sociology and postwar British anthropology.[12] Using surveys to describe individuals' relationships is even newer. An early—perhaps the first—instance of both a network analysis and a network survey was done in a Vermont village in 1936.[13] Since then, researchers have developed, elaborated, and evaluated various survey methods for studying networks.[14] They all, of course, ultimately rely on people *telling* the interviewer about their personal relationships, and such telling can be—as I will shortly review—problematic. Some researchers observe actual behavior—for example, watching which children play with each other, or following people around town to see with whom they spend time. Others uncover social ties in documents—say, records of financial transactions or email logs. Unfortunately, we lack behavioral or documentary evidence about trends in family and friendship and must rely on what Americans have told interviewers.[15] How do we do that, and what are the problems?

Survey researchers generally have asked respondents about their relationships in two ways: one is to ask for global descriptions of their social ties, and the other is to ask for names of particular individuals followed by questions about the named alters. In the first category are questions such as:

"About how many good friends do you have?"[16]

"Is there a friend outside your family with whom you can really share your very private feelings and concerns?"[17]

"How often has someone listened to you talk about your private feelings?"[18]

"How much can you rely on your friends for help if you have a serious problem?"[19]

Some scholars have asked respondents to estimate the number of people whom they know, such as the number with whom they had contact in the previous two years. One estimate is that the average American knows 291 people by sight or by name.[20] Clearly, these are vague questions. The answers depend in part on what respondents consider "knowing" or "friend" to mean, and also on their self-awareness, their desire to impress the interviewer, their patience with the interviews, and their expectations. For example, an elderly widower who talks only to a few people at his favorite lunch spot may claim several "friends" and say that he is satisfied with his social life, while a teenage girl who texts and chats with dozens of other girls daily may feel unpopular and unloved, especially if she has no boyfriend.

Generally and fortunately, people who describe themselves as socially connected in answer to one sort of question—say, how many people they can confide in—tend to describe themselves as socially connected in answer to other network questions—such as how often they see people socially.[21] This reliability is reassuring; its importance is underlined by the fact that, in noteworthy contrast, respondents who report few social connections are *not* likelier than other respondents to score high on measures of how *lonely* they feel. While various network measures tend to crudely separate those with many social ties from those with few, measures of feelings seem to assess a different dimension altogether.[22] However, the correlations between measures of social connection are modest, and that should alert us to methodological considerations—that is, to the specific questions we ask and how we ask them.[23]

The richest sort of network survey questions are the "name-eliciting" or "name-generating" kind—those that ask respondents to list and discuss specific individuals to whom they are connected in specific ways. A classic postwar study employing this method was Elihu Katz and Paul Lazarsfeld's *Personal Influence.* In 1945–1946, researchers asked about eight hundred women in Decatur, Illinois, many questions along the lines of "Do you know anyone around here who keeps up with the news and whom you can trust to let you know what is really going on?" and "Have you recently been asked your advice about which [motion] pictures to see. . . . By whom?" Interviewers then asked respondents to provide the names and addresses, or at least some information, about each person they had mentioned.[24] Over the next few decades, other scholars adapted and elaborated on this approach.[25] In 1985 the General Social Survey asked the question eliciting the names of people with whom interviewees had discussed "important matters."[26]

Name-eliciting questions tend to ask for names in one of three ways, corresponding to the conceptual distinctions I made earlier: respondents name those with whom they have actual or anticipated "exchanges," such as people from whom they get advice (as in the Decatur study) or people whom they accompany to dinner; those who fit role labels like "child," "friend," or "coworker"; or those to whom they feel attached, such as the people "you are close to" or "who are important to you."[27] One survey item used by Edward Laumann in 1965, requesting the names of "the three men who are your closest friends and whom you see most often," combined the role label "friend," the sentiment "closest," and the behavior of "seeing often," although the key criterion was the role label "friend." A few studies suggest that exchange-based questions probably yield the fullest and most valid lists of respondents' personal ties.[28] Fortunately, studies also suggest that the different approaches tend to elicit similar names when those named people are particularly important and active in respondents' lives.

Network analysts have noted the limitations of the name-eliciting method. It takes much time and effort for respondents to provide a relatively full and accurate census of their relationships.[29] It also depends heavily on respondents' memories, which are certainly fallible. (Recall that many could not remember an "important matters" discussion.) In the end, the specific people whom respondents name vary by question wording, by time, by mood, and such. Today a respondent might name

Sally as one of the people who could pick up her mail, but tomorrow she might forget to name Sally and add Jim to her answer. Yet the general list we get of respondents' important ties and the general descriptions we get of those people—say, what proportion are relatives, how far away most of them live—are roughly consistent from one time to the next. In that way, the method provides reliable *aggregate* descriptions—and the more name-eliciting questions used, and the more different kinds, probably the more valid those aggregate descriptions tend to be.[30]

For all the careful attention that researchers have given to the name-eliciting techniques, the brute fact is that the bulk of the data that have been used to describe changes in Americans' social lives—say, the data analyzed by Putnam in *Bowling Alone*—and that I use here are both much cruder and much less well researched. We have to rely on questions such as: "Now, how about friends. About how many close friends do you have these days? Would you say that you have no close friends, one or two, three to five, six to ten, or more than that?" . . . "To the statement 'Our whole family usually eats dinner together,' answer from (1) 'definitely disagree' . . . to (6) 'definitely agree' " . . . "How often do you have any other contact with your mother besides visiting, either by telephone or letter?"

These are difficult questions for respondents to answer precisely, even if they really try. Answers are also shaped by factors such as how people present themselves to the interviewer (if the interview is face-to-face) or just to themselves. Consider that in 1987 almost three-fourths of interviewees said "yes" when asked whether "your parents-in-law are the kind of people you would choose for friends if you were not related to them"—a dubiously high proportion if only because the parents-in-law were about the same age as the respondents' own parents.[31] Respondents' answers also depend on how well they understand the language of the question; how they interpret the terms ("friend," for example, is a quite squishy label[32]); interviewer facial or voice expressions; how the question is introduced (compare the preface "Everybody gets together with friends regularly . . ." to "Most people have just a couple of very close friends . . ."); and so forth.

Assessing change over time in the answers raises yet more issues. One problem is variation in question wording. How can we tell whether people's networks changed if the questions used to measure those networks changed?[33] Altering the answer options also matters—say, whether interviewers or questionnaires explicitly present "never" as a possible answer to a question asking how often respondents visited with their best friends.[34] And even when the words of a question stay the same, its meaning can still change over time. For instance, starting in 1994, Pew Center interviewers asked Americans, "Yesterday, did you . . . call a friend or relative just to talk?" By the 2000s, had their respondents come to understand "call" as including text-, instant-, or video-messaging as well as tele-phoning? Variation in the location of the question within the interview can also shape answers. For example, a question about whether respondents have someone who could help them in a crisis following questions about how depressed they feel might well get different replies than if it followed questions about respondents' favorite hobbies.[35]

Even when the survey wording and context stay the same, the wider context can change in ways that nudge respondents toward one answer or another. Historical events like 9/11 or economic downturns can shape social life and feelings. (In chapter 6, we will see that reports of feeling lonely seem to respond to national tragedies.) Also, people's answers can reflect the season of the year: social activities tend to increase during good weather and holiday periods.[36]

Changes in procedures can affect results. In the years covered here, many polling organizations moved from in-person surveys to over-the-telephone and then automated, over-the-Internet surveys. Telephone interviewing has become increasingly problematic as more people, especially the young and socially active, disconnect their landlines and rely only on cell phones. How survey organizations draw their samples has changed over time, and those changes could create false trends or conceal real trends in personal ties. Response rates—the percentage of the randomly targeted respondents who actually complete the interview—vary greatly from one survey organization to another and have been generally dropping over time. Through the mid-2000s, estimates appear to be that the consequences of this declining cooperation for most survey answers are modest (except perhaps when small differences have big consequences, as in close elections).[37] We do not know if and how these methodological trends have affected responses to questions about personal ties. And finally, even processing errors can creep in that, if undetected by close examination (and not all can be discovered), may alter findings.[38]

In sum, there is a lot of "noise" in surveys about personal ties. Much of that noise is random and evens out in the long run. Even so, the noise must make us wary of any single result or even any pair of results.

Subjectivity

A reader might ask: if getting accurate descriptions of people's actual personal networks is so difficult and error-fraught—especially for making comparisons over decades—why not just look at how Americans feel about their social relationships? The simple answer, as I briefly noted earlier, is that the realities of people's ties and their feelings about those ties are not strongly associated. Whether Americans *felt* more or less isolated from 1970 to 2010 is different from whether they *were* more or less socially isolated. There are important reasons to care about those feel-ings. For example, studies suggest that a person's health may depend more on whether he or she feels loved and supported by others than on whether he or she really is loved and supported.[39] Although the focus of this study is on estimating trends in actual social relations, it is worth-while exploring what we know about people's subjective assessments. I briefly address two sorts of feelings: loneliness and trust.

Operationally, many researchers define "loneliness" in terms of answers to questions such as (1) "How often do you feel that you lack companionship?"; (2) "How often do you feel left out?"; (3) "How often do you feel that there are people you can turn to?"; and (4) "How often do you feel that there are people who really understand you?" Research subjects who tend to say "sometimes" or "often" to questions like the first two and "rarely" or "never" to questions like the second two are consid-ered people who suffer from loneliness.[40] Such people tend also to more often report being alone and to report having smaller circles of friends and confidants. Importantly, however, that association is weak. It is so weak that researchers consider loneliness to be a separate matter from actual alone-ness.[41] We know little about trends over time in Americans' feelings of loneliness. In chapter 6, we take a look at a few fragments of data.

Many surveys have asked, and many scholars have analyzed, this ques-tion: "Generally speaking, would you say that most people can be trusted, or that you can't be too careful in dealing with people?"[42] The percentage of American respondents who chose the trust option fell from over 50 per-cent in the 1960s to about 40 percent by the 1990s, mainly because in each decade fewer young Americans picked the trust option than did Americans of earlier generations. People tend to stick with their youthful worldviews for the rest of their lives.[43] Some scholars suggest that the decline reflects Americans' increasing experience of untrustworthy behav-ior from people around them, who have become, for example, less honest or law-abiding[44]; others that it reflects Americans' fearful reactions to the national traumas of assassination, war, political scandal, and urban vio-lence[45]; some that it reflects Americans' reactions to increasing cultural diversity, immigration, and integration[46]; and yet others that it reflects changes in the personalities of Americans, who have become suspicious and untrustworthy individuals.[47]

Since the trust question asks respondents to think about people *in general*—in effect, to think about strangers rather than about family and friends—it is peripheral to the topic of this book. However, to the extent that the question may in fact reflect something about the personalities of respondents or their sense of interpersonal estrangement, it might contribute to understanding some changes since the 1960s. I revisit this trend in chapter 6.

Surveys and "Harder" Social Indicators

Skeptics argue that surveys are too flawed to reveal the actual social lives of Americans. They note that many people do not answer surveys, many of those who do answer do not understand the questions, and even many of those who do then answer dishonestly. (There are even gasbags who proudly announce that they lie on surveys, including the U.S. census, and therefore *know* that all survey results are fraudulent.) No one is more aware than professional survey researchers of surveys' problems and limitations, from faked interviews to the traps in wording. Many studies of and guides on these issues are available.[48] Nonetheless, properly done surveys converge on basic results, and their findings are typically validated—most commonly in election polls—or at least provide estimates of their errors.

The final argument for surveys is that there is no alternative—not if we hope to say something accurate about the general population. Each of us lives in a parochial social world, one in which just about "everyone" votes the same way, believes in the same things, enjoys the same pastimes, and so on. Extrapolating to all Americans the experiences of, say, rural Kansans, yields a sharply different conclusion than extrapolating from, say, the lives of Manhattan's Upper East Side residents. (Even the intrepid ethnographer can, at best, add only two or three additional, narrow perspectives to his or her personal worldview.) Survey research, for all its flaws, is how we try to gain a satellite picture of the country. The flaws of surveys, however, remind us that the data are rough approximations. When a respondent, for example, says that he or she has four "close friends," we do not take that as a "truth." What we do understand is that this respondent claims more friends than the respondent who claimed one or two.

Perhaps there are some sorts of "harder" social indicators that could be used. Ironically, most such data are themselves drawn from surveys, even if much larger surveys than the ones I use here, like the U.S. census. Others may be drawn from administrative records. In any case, we will not find easy answers in censuslike surveys. Take the following example.

Commentators point to living arrangements when discussing personal relationships—or the absence thereof.[49] They have reported the great increase in the percentage of homes with only one resident, from 13 percent of households in 1960 to 28 percent in 2008.[50] (If we count *people* instead of housing units, the rise is from 4 percent of Americans living alone in 1960 to 11 percent in 2008—15 percent of those age twenty or older.[51]) Three distinct developments have contributed to this change. Most important is the extended longevity and independence of the widowed. They used to be much fewer in number and commonly lived with their children, but now they live longer and are more likely to live independently. Research indicates that most of them prefer that independence. Today's solo dwellers also include young adults living on their own during the transition from their parents' home to a now-more-delayed marriage. (Some, by the way, are technically counted as singles but are living with a partner who is officially listed in another household.) And the third group is the increasing number of divorced and not-yet-remarried men.[52]

The most critical issue for us is this: how alone are people who live alone? Clearly, they usually have no one to wake up with and come home to. But research suggests that, on average, they have more social connections outside their homes than do people who live with others.[53] (Think of the socially active single compared to the housebound mother of an infant.) We cannot take the "hard" data on living arrangements as evidence about people's overall social involvement.

Another tactic is to consider data on purported *correlates* of social connection or disconnection—phenomena we might imagine either cause or result from the kind of social engagement that people have. One possible correlate, for example, is residential mobility. The notion that people who move about have fewer close social ties is central to many discussions of isolation in America, but it is wrong.[54] Another often presumed proxy is marital status, particularly the assumption that the divorced are isolated. Again, if there is a connection, it is pretty weak.[55] As a final example, could something like the suicide rates of a population indicate the state of social ties in that population? There is the long-standing assumption, going back at least to Durkheim, that people with weaker social support are at higher risk of attempting suicide. True, but the connection is hardly strong enough to provide a solid indicator.[56] For the record, the trend for suicides in the United States since 1960 is, overall, pretty flat, although that partly reflects two contradictory developments—a decline in suicide rates among the elderly and an increase in suicide rates among young men into the mid-1990s (and a decline afterward).[57]

In sum, until someone devises some more accurate surveyor of people—say, an electronic spying gadget that tracks all virtual and in-person social contacts—we must rely on the sorts of surveys used in this book. They are only rough approximations, to be sure, but nonetheless they tell us much more than we presume to know.

The Strategy for This Book

In the best of all possible social science worlds, we would have the same sort of rich, consistent, long-running data about Americans' personal relationships that we have about, say, the makeup of American households.

A bit more realistically, we would want to periodically ask nationally representative samples of Americans a broad set of questions about the people with whom they are connected. The Dutch have initiated something along these lines.[58] Instead, we have a diverse set of surveys done at a variety of times in a variety of ways asking a variety of questions about a variety of aspects of a variety of respondents' relationships.

Still, the issue motivating this book is sufficiently compelling and the data are sufficiently indicative. Specifically, I try to assess change in how many relatives and friends Americans reported being connected to; how much contact Americans reported with family and friends; whether Americans had people whom they thought they could rely on in cases of need; and how Americans felt about their relationships—how satisfied, how lonely, how needy. Note that measures of Americans' civic activities, such as belonging to clubs, voting, or serving as a community leader, are *not* included in this list. These are important matters, but different ones.[59] In Robert Putnam's Yiddish, we are looking for the *shmoozers* rather than the *machers*.[60]

Criteria, Conventions, and Caveats

In canvassing the literature and original data, I used a few rules of thumb as I looked for:

- *Research reports and surveys on nationally representative samples of Americans that cover at least portions of the forty years from 1970 through 2009.* On occasion I take advantage of data that go back yet another decade or two.

- *Surveys posing questions that, at least on the surface, ask about important dimensions of personal relationships.* Such questions include, for example, "How often do you visit your mother?" "How many close friends would you say you have?" and "If you needed help around the home, who would you turn to first?"

- *Surveys that repeat the same question in identical or almost identical terms.* The eminent sociologist Otis Dudley Duncan once said, according to the eminent sociologist Michael Hout, that, "if you want to measure change, don't change the measure." Although circumstances can challenge this principle—when, for example, words change meaning, such as happened with the word "gay"—it remains a critical guide.

- *Results at least five or more years apart between 1970 and 2009.* The ideal is a question asked, say, every few years over the entire period. There are few like that.[61]

- *Surveys that provide estimates at several points.* When we look at only two or three times, the vagaries of any period or poll can mislead us about trends (although I have had to relax this criterion in a few cases).

- *Studies and surveys we can assume are of reasonable quality and accuracy.*

Concretely, I gathered the data by:

- *Canvassing the research literature for published findings.*

- *Exploring data repositories for descriptive results*—mainly the Inter-University Consortium for Political and Social Research at the University of Michigan; the Roper Center's Public Opinion Archives at the University of Connecticut; the Gallup Poll's "Gallup Brain" database; and the Polling the Nations database.[62] In these cases, I simply use the marginals—the distribution of answers to the questions by the year the questions were asked.

- *Running statistical analyses on a few survey data sets.* The main one is the GSS, conducted by the National Opinion Research Center; since 1972, the GSS has been the most comprehensive and exacting survey on topics of sociological interest.[63] I also analyzed the DDB Needham surveys relied on by Putnam in *Bowling Alone,* extending the time period beyond the last year Putnam could cover; the Roper survey data compiled by Henry Brady and his colleagues[64]; the World Values Survey; the American National Election Survey; and the two National Comorbidity Studies (for more detail, see appendix A).

Finally, the presentation and discussion of the data largely follow, although not slavishly, several conventions:

- The question driving this book is descriptive: How did Americans' relationships change over forty years? Explaining why changes occurred—or did not occur—is another, more complex task. Although I occasionally address such questions, *the focus of this book is on the "what," not the "why."* Put more technically, the book largely reports changes in marginals.

- Because of the inevitable ambiguities and errors in survey research, where possible *I try to pool several data series and thereby generate a consensus about any trend.*

- For similar reasons, a statistical difference is not a real change unless we see a substantial contrast—say, at least five to ten percentage points over at least ten years. *Statistical significance does not suffice.*[65]

- With time displayed in most of the tables and figures in this book as the full spread between 1970 through 2010, even if the data under inspection cover only a brief segment of those four decades, *any short-term patterns are put into context.*

- Throughout the book, *I try to separate data about relatives from data about nonfamily relationships.* It is not always possible. Many survey questions, for example, ask about discussions that respondents have with "family and friends." However, as I pointed out earlier, kinship is a critical distinction. Survey items that conflate kin and nonkin are discussed in the sections on nonkin.

Having done more than enough throat-clearing, I turn to the data.

═ Chapter 3 ═

Counting People: Family

THIS CHAPTER turns to the evidence on the trends between 1970 and 2010 in the volume of Americans' social involvement. It addresses their connections specifically with relatives; the next chapter addresses their connections with nonrelatives. Some of the available surveys posed questions that lumped family and friends together—for example, asking whether respondents had chatted with "friends *or* family" the previous day. I discuss those surveys in chapter 4.

How Many Relatives?

The first step is to clarify what may have changed in the simple, demographic *availability* of relatives. In the end, what probably matters to people is how many relatives they have with whom they share their lives, not what proportion of their relatives share their lives. The size of an individual's family, at minimum, puts a ceiling on the number of kin he or she might call on. It also probably affects the strain that relatives might feel. For example, how many adult children and siblings an elderly person has partly determines how likely he or she is to get help—and how much providing that help burdens each child or sibling.

Americans in 2010 had fewer relatives than Americans did in 1970. Because they married substantially later and because more of them divorced, and despite the fact that they were less likely to be widowed, these twenty-first-century Americans were about ten percentage points less likely to be married than Americans of the 1970s.[1] More Americans than before, however, cohabited in marriagelike arrangements. Treating those partners as if they were spouses deflates the change, so that, in net, about 5 percent fewer American adults at the end of the period had a live-in partner (of either sex).[2] Of all the family and friends who could matter to an adult, spouses by far matter the most, socially and psychologically.[3] By this profound if simple fact alone, we would expect Americans in the 2000s to have a diminished personal network compared to Americans of the 1970s.

The birthrate in the United States dropped for over a century before World War II, rose sharply during the baby boom—roughly 1947 to 1960—and then plunged again. (In the 1950s, the birthrate was about 25 per 1,000 Americans; in the late 1970s, it was about 15 per 1,000.[4]) Extended longevity provided a counterbalance, but the longer lives of the aged were not nearly as great a factor in determining how many relatives a person had.[5] Americans' kin shrank in number, and the GSS provides some rough estimates of that shrinkage. In the 1970s, GSS respondents reported having ever had, on average, 4.2 siblings. In the 2000s, the average was down to 3.6 siblings. (If we restrict our sample to respondents between the ages of twenty-five and sixty in order to simplify matters,[6] the decline is not as sharp—going from an average of 4.0 siblings in the 1970s to an average of 3.6 in the 2000s.) The trend is linear.[7] Similarly, GSS respondents' answers to the question about the number of children they ever had shows a decline—from an average of 2.2 in the 1970s to 1.9 in the 2000s.[8] (The number of children Americans think is *ideal* for a family dropped by about a half-child, from an average of three to around two and a half, between 1970 and 1990 and then leveled off afterwards.[9]) No surprise, then, that the number of Americans living together in one home dropped—from an average of 3.1 people per American household in 1970 to an average of 2.6 in 1990 and later. From 1970 to around 1990, the percentage of Americans, adults and children, who shared a household with at least four other people fell from 38 to 21 percent, where it stayed for the next twenty years.[10]

These marriage and parenting trends have multiplier effects. Aside from the issue—or non-issue—of children, the unmarried do not have in-laws. Individuals who have fewer siblings and fewer children per sibling also have fewer cousins, nephews, nieces, and grandchildren, and the next generation has fewer uncles and aunts. A rough, back-of-the-envelope calculation suggests that middle-aged Americans in the 2000s had during their lives perhaps three-fourths as many *blood* kin as did middle-aged Americans in the 1970s.[11] Greater longevity preserves more living connections among parents, children, grandparents, and grandchildren, but that trend, especially since about 1960, was weaker than the decline in marrying and parenting. Another countervailing trend, the "blending" of families by divorce and remarriage, increased the number of Americans' stepsiblings and in-laws, but remarriage rates, although rising, did not keep up with divorce rates.[12] A one-fourth decline in the number of living relatives is too high an estimate, but even a one-eighth decline in the number of kin the average American had would be noteworthy.

Some scholars have described the trend as "beanpole families": more generations are alive at the same time—children, parents, grandparents—but there are fewer relatives in each generation. The consequences for social support are mixed. On the one hand, Americans have fewer kin overall to call upon, but on the other hand, they face less competition for support from immediate kin. Fewer adult children have to share assistance (money, babysitting, and so forth) from their elderly parents, and because there are fewer grandchildren, the elderly can get more help from the middle generation.[13]

In sum, Americans in the 2000s generally had fewer relatives with whom they could spend time and upon whom they could hypothetically draw for assistance—or who could draw upon them for assistance—than did Americans forty years earlier. The extent to which Americans in each era actually engaged with their siblings, cousins, nephews, and so on, is a different issue. Perhaps all they needed were a few close kin—in which case, the support might have been just as forthcoming, if not more so.

Nuclear Family Togetherness

Americans had smaller families in the 2000s than in the 1970s. And with more single-parent families and more elderly people living independently, Americans shared a home with fewer kin in the 2000s than in the 1970s. Did the activities and intimacy of those nuclear families change?

Many pollsters have focused on the extent to which families share meals. (Historians have noted that the family dinner is a relatively modern, late-nineteenth-century invention, but it certainly has a powerful pull on contemporary Americans.[14]) Yet the topic has not been handled systematically over the years, with the exception of a major commercial survey. That survey requires particular note. The DDB Needham company's mail-in market poll taps a volunteer panel. It is a relatively unusual survey to use for academic analysis; its procedures seem to violate the conventional standards. Nonetheless, Robert Putnam employed it and defended its validity in *Bowling Alone*; other scholars have also used it. In spite of its particularities, the basic results it provides—say, on how many Americans smoke, or how many go hunting—seem to match those of high-quality standard surveys.[15] I use it here and later in this book.

Figure 3.1 shows the percentage of DDB respondents from 1977 through 2003 who agreed with the statement, "Our whole family usually eats dinner together." This figure roughly replicates that reported by Putnam, with a few adjustments, notably taking the data into the twenty-first century.[16] Although, for technical reasons (see figure 3.1 note), the figure presents one set of answers for the whole sample from 1985 on and another set of answers from 1977 through 1998 for respondents who

**Figure 3.1   Respondents Whose Families Usually Eat Dinner Together—
DDB Needham**

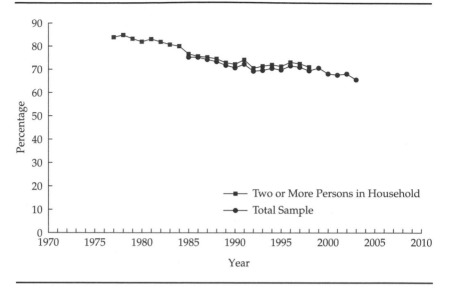

Source: Author's compilation based on data from DDB Needham, variable name "famdin."
Question: "Our whole family usually eats dinner together," with six-point response scale: (1) definitely disagree, (2) generally disagree, (3) moderately disagree, (4) moderately agree, (5) generally agree, and (6) definitely agree.
Notes: (1) I show here and elsewhere a line for the total sample, 1985 to 2003, and a line for only respondents in two-person households, 1977 to 1998, for two reasons. First, before 1985, DDB sought only married respondents. Later, starting in 1985, it sought a full sample, including the unmarried, and asked all respondents this question, even those who lived alone. Second, the two-person household series cannot be continued beyond 1998 because the microdata are not available for analysis (at least not to me) and I had to rely on published marginals. (2) From 1985 to 1998 about 52 percent of respondents in one-person households "agreed" with the statement, compared to 73 percent for other respondents. It is not clear what that answer means in a one-person household and what it implies for the answers of other respondents.

shared their households with at least one other person (that is, this set ignores respondents who lived alone), the trend is nevertheless quite clear: downward.[17]

Other surveys have been more precise, asking respondents how many days a week they usually eat as a family or how often they did so in the previous week. But these surveys cover many fewer years. Figure 3.2 presents the results from Gallup's question about respondents' usual practice—"How many nights a week out of seven does

Figure 3.2   Respondents Whose Families Eat Together at Home, by How Often—Gallup

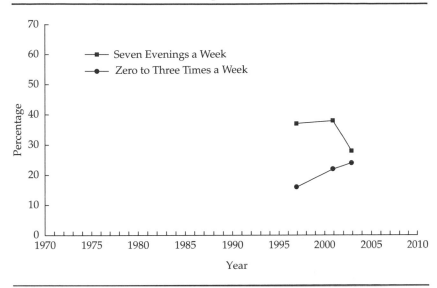

Sources: Author's compilation based on data from iPoll, USGALLUP.97FB24.R35; Kiefer (2004).
Question: "How many nights a week out of seven does your family eat dinner together at home?"
Note: This sample includes only respondents from households with children under age eighteen.

your family eat dinner together at home?"—and figure 3.3 presents the results from the CBS/*New York Times* poll's question—"In the last seven days, how many evenings did *most* of your family eat together?" Finally on this point, figure 3.4 presents a series that asked parents about whether they and their children ate the "main meal" on weekdays "as a family unit—that is, parents and some or all of the children." Although all the polls shown in this set (and the next ones through figure 3.11) were conducted by the Roper organization, we have different samples taken at different times in somewhat different ways, so multiple lines are displayed.

The results in figures 3.1 to 3.4 are "noisy," but there is a downward trend.[19] All of the data here—and results reported by others[20]—point toward at least a moderate decline since 1970 in families having meals at home together (even as the number of people who would have to be corralled to the table declined). A 2009 survey pursued this topic by asking respondents why they sometimes did not eat as a family. The most

**Figure 3.3   Respondents Who Ate Together with Their Family
Last Week, by How Often—CBS/*New York Times***

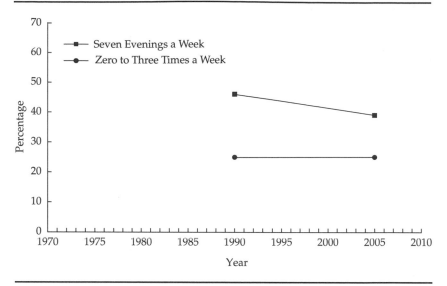

Source: Author's compilation based on data from iPoll, CBS/*New York Times* poll,
USCBSNYT.NOV90.R16 and USCBS.112005.R63.
Question: "In the last seven days, how many evenings did most of your family eat dinner
together?"
Note: This sample includes only respondents from households with children under age
eighteen.

common explanations were that "people are working late" and, among
parents, that "kids have activities that conflict with dinner."[21]

In 1998 about half of Americans polled predicted that "families sitting down to eat dinner together" will have "pretty much disappeared" by
2028.[22] Although the trends we see do not imply disappearance—and other
fragmentary data suggest that the trend flattened out in the 2000s[23]—they
are consistent with that sentiment. Another set of results from the Roper
polls, however, provide a different perspective on eating together—how
often did families eat *out* together (figure 3.5)? The same caution about the
varying samples applies. Between 1974 and 1990, more American parents
reported that they ate *out* frequently or often as "a family unit." The point
for 1994 reverses the trend, but it is a particularly atypical poll.[24] It would
seem, then, that the decline in the number of family meals applied only to
meals *at home.*[25]

A handful of surveys conducted by the Roper organization between
1974 and 1991 asked about several sorts of family activities. Figures

Figure 3.4 **Respondents Who Frequently Have Weekday Meals As a Family—Roper**

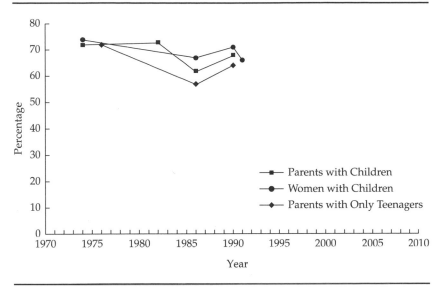

Sources: Author's compilation. Roper conducted the 1974 poll for Virginia Slims (iPoll: USROPER.74VASL.Q45B) and the 1982 poll for the Television Broadcast Authority (iPoll: USROPER.040083.R17A). The 1976, 1986, and 1990 polls came via Brady et al. (2000).
Question. "I'm going to name some different kinds of things, and for each one, would you tell me how often you do it as a family unit—that is, parents and some or all of the children? First, how often do you have the main meal together [stated explicitly in 1974 and 1986; 'on weekdays']—frequently, fairly often, not too often, seldom, or never?"
Notes: (1) "Weekday" is not explicitly stated in the 1982 version. (2) The results for the 1974 poll are presented in the source by gender; this figure averages the male and female percentages. (3) The sample in some polls includes only respondents with children age seven to seventeen or eighteen.

3.4 and 3.5 show answers to the questions specifically about meals. Figures 3.6 to 3.11 show the patterns for some other questions. As before with these polls, we have a variety of ways of matching them up. A gloss on the results suggests that frequently doing activities "as a family unit" at home declined, while trends for doing other activities were roughly flat. The 1990s data—in particular, Putnam's reports of the 1997 points—stand out in showing notable drops. (Generally, respondents shifted from saying "frequently" to saying "fairly often"; the proportions saying "not too often," "seldom," or "never" changed little.) The trends are neither uniform nor dramatic, but taken together, they point to a moderate decline in reports of families doing activities together.[26]

**Figure 3.5   Respondents Who Frequently or Often Eat Out
As a Family—Roper**

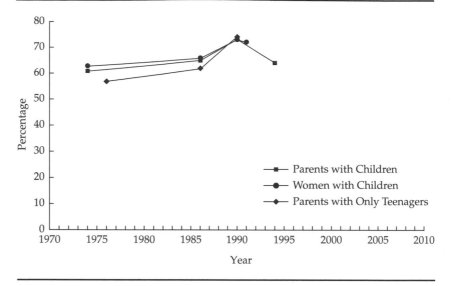

Sources: Author's compilation. Roper conducted the 1974 poll for Virginia Slims (iPoll: USROPER.74VASL.Q45B) and the 1982 poll for the Television Broadcast Authority (iPoll: USROPER.040083.R17A). The 1976, 1986, and 1990 polls came via Brady et al. (2000).
Question: "I'm going to name some different kinds of things, and for each one, would you tell me how often you do it as a family unit—that is, parents and some or all of the children? How often do you . . . go out to eat together . . . frequently, fairly often, not too often, seldom, or never?"
Notes: (1) The 1986 and 1990 values for "women with children" are based on the female subsample in the Brady et al. (2000) data. The 1976 point is not comparable because only parents of children seven to seventeen were included then. (2) The 1974 poll results are reported for men and women separately; the overall results represent a weighted average of the genders. (3) The 1991 survey was of women only.

Yet time-budget studies suggest that American parents were spending *more* time with their children after 2000 than they had spent in the decades before.[27] (In time-budget studies, researchers ask a representative sample of people to keep track of their activities, who they do them with, when they do them, and for how long.) How can these two sets of findings be reconciled? It is likely that, with more mothers working longer hours and with more children engaged in extracurricular activities outside the home, parents less often coordinated common "family activities" such as meals, visits, or even television-watching—but nonetheless spent more time accompanying their children to their playdates, sports practices, and so forth, as well as taking them along on parental trips such as grocery shopping. In fact, a few of the Roper polls (not shown here) also asked about

Figure 3.6   Respondents Who Frequently Entertain Friends or Relatives As a Family—Roper

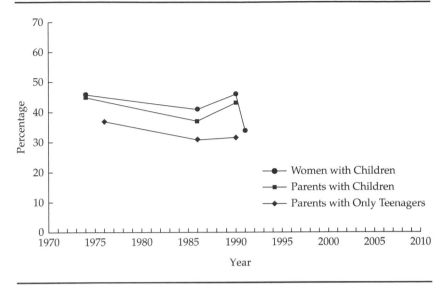

Sources: For full source information see chapter 3, note 18.
Question: "(I'm going to name some different kinds of things, and for each one, would you tell me how often you do it as a family unit—that is, parents and some or all of the children?) . . . How often do you entertain friends or family at home together—frequently, fairly often, not too often, seldom, or never?"
Notes: (1) The 1986 and 1990 values for "women with children" are based on the female subsample in the Brady et al. (2000) data. (2) The 1976 point is not comparable because only parents of children ages seven to seventeen were included.

shopping for food as "a family unit"; reports of frequently doing so *rose* substantially from the mid-1970s to 1990.[28] Changes may also depend on the age of the children. One study compared surveys of high schoolers in "Middletown" (Muncie, Indiana) in 1999 to those in 1977; the more recent cohort reported spending less time with parents than did the 1977 respondents, a decrease that the authors attributed to divorce and mothers' employment.[29] Americans' perceptions of what has changed are in line with the evidence from time-budget studies. In a 1987 Gallup poll, 65 percent of respondents said that "parents spending more time with their children" was "gaining favor and popularity."[30]

Finally, spouses: Paul Amato and his colleagues report major declines in spouses doing various activities together—although no decline in marital happiness or stability. Suzanne Bianchi and her colleagues found that American parents spent 20 to 25 percent fewer minutes a day

**Figure 3.7   Respondents Who Frequently Visit Friends or Relatives
As a Family—Roper**

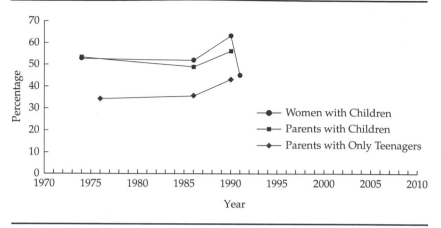

Sources: For full source information see chapter 3, note 18.
Question: "I'm going to name some different kinds of things, and for each one, would you
tell me how often you do it as a family unit—that is, parents and some or all of the
children? . . . [How often do you] visit friends or family together?"
Notes: See notes to figure 3.6.

**Figure 3.8   Respondents Who Frequently Do Fun Things
As a Family—Roper**

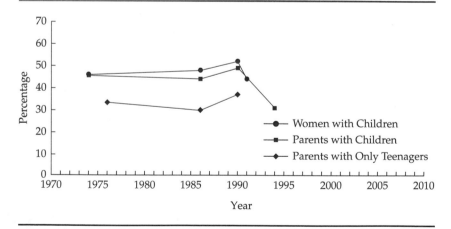

Sources: For full source information see chapter 3, note 18.
Question: "I'm going to name some different kinds of things, and for each one, would you
tell me how often you do it as a family unit—that is, parents and some or all of the
children? . . . [How often do you] do things together for fun and recreation (go to movies,
events, picnics, etc.)?"
Note: See notes to figure 3.6.

Figure 3.9   Respondents Who Frequently Attend Religious Services As a Family—Roper

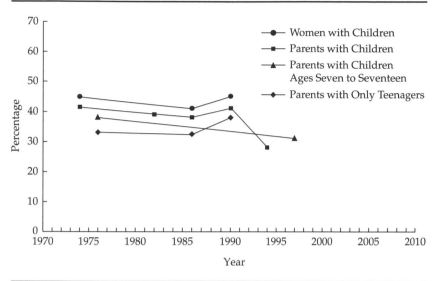

Sources: For full source information see chapter 3, note 18.
Question: "I'm going to name some different kinds of things, and for each one, would you tell me how often you do it as a family unit—that is, parents and some or all of the children? . . . [How often do you] attend religious services together?"
Notes: (1) See notes to figure 3.6. (2) The question was not asked in 1991.

with their spouses in 2000 than in 1975, and they argue that this was a major way, along with letting housework slide, that parents in 2000 were able to spend more time with their children while working longer hours.[31]

In sum, the fragments of evidence we have point to nuclear families doing less together as a family group, especially at-home activities (eating meals, entertaining, watching television, talking), but doing out-of-the-home activities as a group (eating out, visiting, doing "fun things") as often as in the past, or perhaps more often (with the exception of attending religious services). Given the time-budget evidence, it appears that family schedules were bending to mothers' work and children's extracurricular activities.

Contact with Kin

This section presents the evidence on how often Americans reported getting together with relatives outside of the nuclear family. In 1986 and 2002, the GSS asked roughly comparable specific questions: "How

Figure 3.10   Respondents Who Frequently Watch TV As a Family—Roper

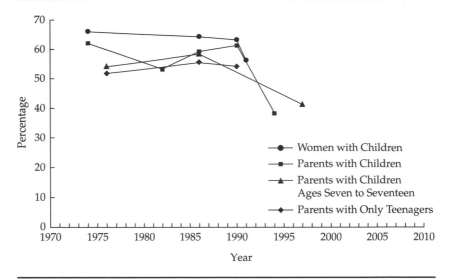

- ● Women with Children
- ■ Parents with Children
- ▲ Parents with Children
  Ages Seven to Seventeen
- ◆ Parents with Only Teenagers

Sources: For full source information see chapter 3, note 18.
Question: "I'm going to name some different kinds of things, and for each one, would you tell me how often you do it as a family unit—that is, parents and some or all of the children? . . . [How often do you] watch TV together?"
Note: See notes to figure 3.6.

Figure 3.11   Respondents Who Frequently Sit and Talk As a Family—Roper

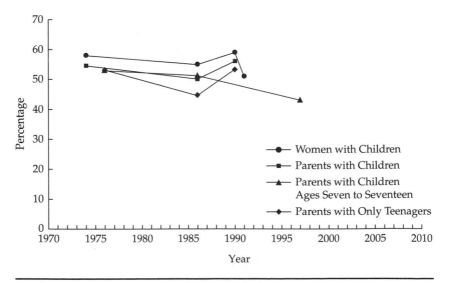

- ● Women with Children
- ■ Parents with Children
- ▲ Parents with Children
  Ages Seven to Seventeen
- ◆ Parents with Only Teenagers

Sources: For full source information see chapter 3, note 18.
Question: "I'm going to name some different kinds of things, and for each one, would you tell me how often you do it as a family unit—that is, parents and some or all of the children? . . . [How often do you] sit and talk together?"
Note: See notes to figure 3.6.

Figure 3.12   Respondents Who See Parents Weekly or More Often, by Which Parent—GSS

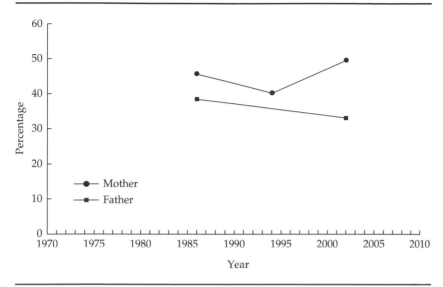

Source: Author's compilation based on data from GSS items "mavisit," "mavisit1," "pavisit," "pavisit1."
Questions: Mothers, 1986 and 1994, for respondents who report that their mothers are alive: "How often do you see or visit your mother?" Mothers, 2002, after questions about other relatives: "And what about your mother? How often do you see or visit her?" (Mother not being alive is one answer.) Father questions were similar in 1986 and 2002, but the 1994 survey did not ask about fathers.
Notes: (1) Respondents who lived with the parent are excluded. (2) For the 1986 to 2002 comparisons, note that the sequence of relatives asked about differs, with parents coming toward the end in 2002. (3) In 1986 the questions were preceded by a question asking if the parent was alive, but not in 2002. (4) The 1986 questions were asked face-to-face, while the 1994 and 2002 questions were on self-administered questionnaires (SAQs). (5) The 1994 survey asked only the mother question.

often do you see or visit your mother (father)?" In 1994 the GSS asked about mothers only, and in a slightly different format. Figure 3.12 shows the percentage of respondents in 1986 and 2002 who said that they saw their parents at least once a week[32] (including parents who lived with the respondents or slicing the response categories in other ways makes little change in the results). One noteworthy methodological difference between the surveys is that in 1986 interviewers directly posed the question to respondents, but in 2002 the question was part of a self-administered questionnaire (SAQ) that respondents filled out privately. We might speculate that in 1986 respondents would have been more embarrassed about directly telling interviewers that they

Figure 3.13   Respondents Who Spent Social Evenings Several Times a Month or More with Relatives, Parents, or Siblings—GSS

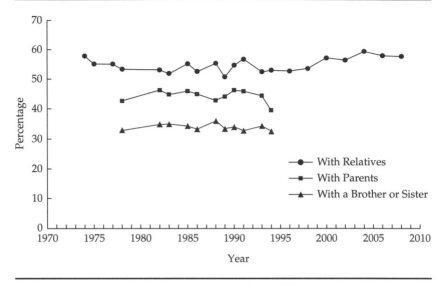

Source: Author's compilation based on data from GSS items "socrel," "socpars," "socsibs."
Questions: "Would you use this card and tell me which answer comes closest to how often you do the following things: (a) Spend a social evening with relatives; . . . (e) your parents; (f) a brother or sister?"

rarely saw their mothers. Survey researchers typically assume that respondents are more forthcoming on sensitive topics in an SAQ.[33] I have no direct evidence, however, of that happening in this case.[34] Respondents reported visiting with their parents about as frequently in both years. The five-point decline in weekly visits with fathers— which is not statistically significant—is largely accounted for by the greater proportion of respondents in 2002 had not lived with their fathers when they were sixteen.[35]

The GSS has for most of four decades asked a set of vaguer questions about getting together with kin, asking respondents how often they spent a "social evening" with "relatives," "your parents," or "a brother or sister." The GSS asked about parents and siblings only between 1978 and 1994. (Interspersed in this set of questions were probes about evenings with nonkin, to which I turn in chapter 4.) Respondents who said that they spent many social evenings with relatives tended to also say that they saw their mothers and fathers often—a reassuring consistency.[36] Figure 3.13 displays the trends (actually, the nontrends): thirty-four

Figure 3.14   Respondents Who Have Contact with Parents Weekly or More Often, by Which Parent—GSS

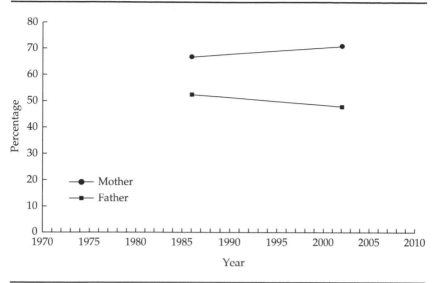

Source: Author's compilation based on data from GSS items "macall," "macall1," "pacall," "pacall1."
Questions: "How often do you have any other contact with your mother (father) besides visiting, either by telephone [or] letter [2002: 'fax or email']?"
Note: See notes for figure 3.12.

years passed, and Americans were consistent in how often they (said that they) saw their relatives.[37] A 1964 survey asking the same question about relatives allows us to add an observation ten years before the first point displayed in figure 3.13: 53 percent of respondents in 1964 said that they saw their relatives for a social evening several times a month or more—a bit lower than the average for the 2000s.[38]

These questions are about face-to-face contact. What about contact through other means? In 1986 the GSS followed up the questions about visiting mothers and fathers (figure 3.12) with questions about *other* contact: "How often do you have any other contact with your mother (father) besides visiting, either by telephone or letter?" In 2002 the GSS expanded the question to: ". . . either by telephone, letter, fax, or email?" The percentages of respondents who had weekly or more frequent contact are shown in figure 3.14. Respondents' reports of contacting their mothers increased a bit—most notably for those who lived over an hour away from their mother[39]—but essentially, little changed.[40] GSS respondents were just about as likely to say *either* that they saw their mother *or* that they called (or emailed) their mother at least once a week in both years: 72 percent in 1986 and 76 percent in 2002 did one or the other or both. Relationships with fathers were more complex. GSS respondents were less likely in 2002 (55 percent) than in 1986 (62 percent) to report either seeing or contacting their fathers once a week. But if we set aside those respondents who at age sixteen had lived apart from their fathers, then there is no difference between the respondents in 1986 (69 percent were in weekly contact) and in 2002 (68 percent). In sum, Americans were as likely in 2002 as in 1986 to be in touch with the parents who had raised them.

One more finding about contact can be added. In the period 1990 to 1992 and again in 2001 to 2003, National Comorbidity Studies conducted large and sophisticated surveys of Americans' health. One question each time asked respondents how often they talked or got together with relatives. The results for the two waves are virtually identical.[41]

Conclusions

We can draw at least a few provisional conclusions. But before doing that, recall the limits of the data: we assume that interviewees' reports are roughly accurate descriptions of American adults' experiences. Surveys systematically fall short in covering Americans at the edges of society—the transient, the homeless, the non-English-speaking, the fugitive, the institutionalized, and any other people who tend to lack social resources. Surveys also have difficulty reaching elites—the residents of penthouses and guarded estates. Still, these problems should have been roughly constant over the period covered here. With these cautions, we can conclude from the surveys reported here and from other studies that American adults of the 2000s compared to American adults of the 1970s:

- Were less likely to be in a couple (about ten percentage points less likely to be married or about five percentage points less likely to have a spouselike partner)
- Had fewer relatives
- Less frequently engaged in at-home activities, including dinner, with the entire nuclear family
- Probably spent at least as much time, if not more, in the company of their children—probably out of the home
- Spent less time with their spouse

- Saw and communicated with their parents about as often (treating fathers who left the family early as a special case)
- Saw other relatives about as often

This pattern of results suggests that Americans were no less committed to their immediate families and other relatives in the 2000s than before, but that they had curtailed some group activities, such as family meals. This conclusion is consistent with an explanation that American families were responding to greater time pressures, especially on women who were working more hours.[42]

Chapter 4

Counting People:
Friends and Others

THIS CHAPTER addresses the same sorts of issues discussed in the previous one about relatives—how many, how often—but about friends and others. Because we can analyze only questions that survey researchers asked over the last forty years, I have to include here items that ask about various categories of social ties, including categories that combine relatives and nonrelatives—such as "About how often do you socialize with close friends, relatives, or neighbors?" I assume that most of the people who came to mind when interviewees were asked such questions were not relatives, and I have therefore put these questions into this chapter.

How Many Nonrelatives Could Americans Be Involved With?

Estimating change in the number of nonkin Americans had available for relationships is even harder than estimating the number of kin. We can think of availability in terms of the "social contexts" in which people participate: the settings that provide individuals with pools of potential colleagues, friends, and acquaintances.[1]

For modern Americans, the main such contexts, aside from kinship, are school, work, neighborhood, and organizations such as churches and clubs. Between 1970 and the 2000s, more Americans passed through college, increasing the number of opportunities to meet and befriend people in the same stage of life.[2] Over that period, a shrinking proportion of adult men were in the labor force (declining from about 81 percent to 75 percent of men age twenty or older), but many more women participated (increasing from about 44 percent to 60 percent of women age twenty or older),[3] suggesting that slightly fewer men but many more women had opportunities to meet and befriend coworkers.

It is harder to estimate trends in Americans' exposure to other contexts. People continued to live in neighborhoods, of course, but wives' growing employment probably reduced their interaction with neighbors and that of their families. Accurately describing trends in Americans' involvement in churches and other organizations is difficult; scholars have fiercely debated those trends since about the mid-1990s. For this book, let us stipulate that a somewhat smaller proportion of adults attended church regularly at the end than at the beginning of this era. (About one-fifth in the 1970s said that they never or rarely attended, and about one-fourth said that in the 2000s.[4]) Similarly, trends suggest a slight decline in Sunday school attendance since the 1950s.[5] And we can stipulate that Americans' membership in formal organizations like veterans' associations and fraternal orders declined after the 1970s. Some experts claim that participation in informal contexts like Bible study groups and support groups made up for declines in formal organizations; this may be true, but we have no solid measures of membership in such informal groups, nor of how many such groups exist.[6]

The rise of the Internet adds yet more complexity to estimating changes in Americans' social contexts. Relatively few Americans, even in the 2000s, "lived" on the Web in the same way that they lived in physical neighborhoods. Yet, according to GSS estimates, about 2 percent of Americans in the early 2000s had made a friendship or other bond with someone they first met on an Internet site.[7] In a 2005 Pew survey, about 1 percent of all respondents said that they had either married or formed a long-term romantic relationship with someone they met on a dating site.[8] The World Wide Web has become an additional, minor but growing, source of new ties.

The Web not only added opportunities for meeting but extended the longevity of existing off-line social contexts and ties. A Facebook group devoted to, say, Elmwood High School's class of 1997 would be one example; never-purged lists of email addresses provide perhaps even more linkages. It is hard to put numbers on how much new technologies to "reach out and touch someone" have kept old ties active. In a 2008 survey, Americans reported having hundreds of days of contact each year through various Internet media and by cell phone with members of their "core network" who lived hundreds of miles away, employing means that were not available in 1970.[9] Internet users certainly *believe* that it has enabled them to expand their ties, and some evidence suggests that they are right.[10] (See chapter 7 for more on the topic of the Internet.)

In 2006 the GSS asked interviewees a question that might crudely get at people's opportunities to form close ties out of casual acquaintance:

On average, about how many people do you have contact with in a typical weekday, including people you live with? We are interested in contact on a one-to-one basis, including everyone with whom you chat, talk, or discuss matters. This can be face-to-face, by telephone, by mail, or on the Internet. Please include only people you know. Please tell me which of the following categories best matches your estimate.

Sixty-two percent of the respondents answered that they had contact with ten or more people on a typical weekday. Those who reported higher numbers were much likelier than those who picked lower estimates to be regularly employed or attending school, to be better educated, and to be white.[11] Extrapolating from—and taking considerable license with—these 2006 data suggests that the rise in educational levels since 1970 provided more opportunities for nonkin ties; that the employment and schooling trends greatly expanded opportunities for women and did little for men[12]; and that the modest decline in the white portion of the population slightly reduced the numbers.

In sum, a rough guess is that, between the 1970s and the 2000s, some of the opportunities that Americans had to make or sustain nonkin ties shrank—notably those with neighbors and, to a lesser extent, those with church and club members—while opportunities to make or sustain other ties grew, such as those with school and college classmates, coworkers (for women), and people met through the Internet (for a small but growing number). Given that this canvass does not get at the more informal aspects of contacts, and given the absence of hard numbers, perhaps we can only conclude, conservatively, that there was probably no net change in opportunities for men and an increase in social opportunities for women.

What the increase in social opportunities for women could mean is that American women in the 2000s made and kept more friends than women in the 1970s did. Or perhaps they could be more selective about who to have as friends, leaving the number about the same. Or it could be that women continued to have about the same number of friends because the expanding pool of potential friends made up for the increasing constraints that women faced in other ways, such as more hours spent working and commuting.[13]

How Many Friends (and Other Ties) Did Americans Actually Have?

We do not have over-time measures that capture the volume of individuals' social ties, including the most intimate and the less intimate.[14] But we do have roughly comparable estimates over time of how many "close friends" Americans claim to have. The comparisons are approximate. This first set of items illustrates the complexities of studying the question of change over time perhaps better than they answer the question.

Figure 4.1   Respondents Claiming Fewer Than Three or More Than Six "Close Friends"—Gallup

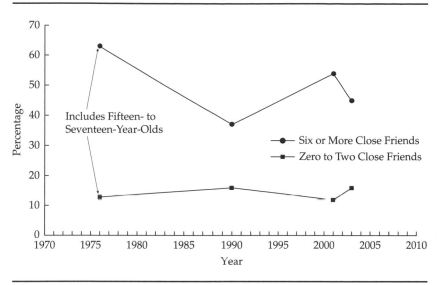

Sources: Author's compilation based on data from iPoll, Gallup Brain.
Question: "Not counting your relatives, about how many close friends would you say you have?"
Notes: (1) Respondents could nominate as many friends as they wished. The iPoll summaries provided collapsed categories. (2) The 1976 poll was conducted by Gallup for the Kettering Foundation with a sample age of fifteen and older. (3) We can expect, from other data, that the youngest respondents gave the highest numbers. (4) This poll seems unavailable for further analysis.

Figures 4.1 through 4.4 present the results for survey questions about numbers of close friends that were replicated (or approximately replicated) over at least a five-year span. The best series we have uses a simple question asked by Gallup from 1976 through 2003, displayed in figure 4.1: "Not counting your relatives, about how many close friends would you say you have?" I have simplified the results into three categories: six or more close friends[15]; zero to two close friends; and three to five close friends, which I do not show for ease of reading. Even here, however, a complexity arises: the 1976 survey included fifteen- to seventeen-year-olds, who, other data suggest, tend to report many friends.

Note, first, that none of these four figures separately displays the zero category—the percentage of respondents who claimed *no* close friends. The reason is that the percentage who reported being friendless is tiny—almost always 5 percent or less—and displays no "action" (no real trend) in any of the four data sets.[16]

Figure 4.2   Respondents Claiming Fewer Than Three or More Than Six "Close Friends"—GSS

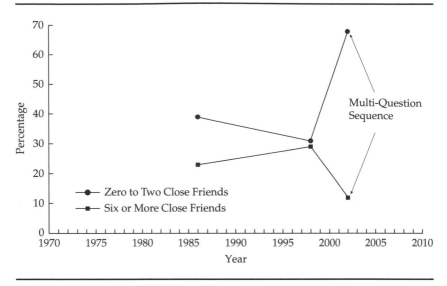

Sources: Author's compilation based on data from GSS items "frinum," "friends," "numfrend," "cowrkfnd," "neifrd," "othfrd." Analyzed online via SDA, University of California–Berkeley, weight = "compwt."

Questions: (A) 1986, "frinum": "Thinking now of close friends—not your husband or wife or partner or family members, but people you feel fairly close to—how many close friends would you say you have?" (B) 1998, "friends" and "numfrend": "Do you have any good friends that you feel close to?"; [if yes:] "About how many good friends do you have?" (C) The 2002 measure was added up from a three-question sequence: (1) "cowrkfnd": "Now we would like to ask you about people you know, other than your family and relatives. The first question is about people at your workplace. Thinking about people at your workplace, how many of them are close friends of yours?"(recoded to zero for those not working) (2) "neifrd": "Thinking now of people who live near you, in your neighborhood or district, how many of these people are close friends of yours?" (3) "othfrd": "How many other close friends do you have—apart from those at work, in your neighborhood, or family members? Think, for instance, of friends at clubs, church, or the like."

Two other studies are relevant to this point. In comparing a 2000 survey to a 1980 survey of married Americans under the age of fifty-five, Paul Amato and his colleagues found an identical 13 percent reporting no "close friends" outside their families.[17] Hua Wang and Barry Wellman, analyzing matching surveys done in 2002 and 2007, found that 5 percent in each year reported no "friends outside of your household . . . that you see or speak to at least once a week."[18] In sum, the data in figures 4.1 to 4.4 and in published work suggest that there was no change in the

Figure 4.3   Respondents Naming Three to Five or Fewer Than Two "Good Friends" They Are "Close To"—GSS

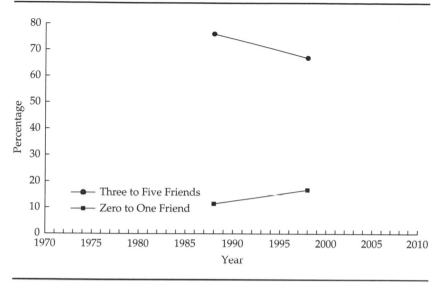

Sources: Author's compilation based on data from GSS items "frndcon1" to "frndcon5." Analyzed online via SDA, University of California–Berkeley, weight = "compwt."
Question: "Many people have some good friends they feel close to. Who are your good friends (other than your spouse)?"
Note. No explicit variable for the number of friends that respondents named in 1988 and 1998 appears in the GSS archives, because the question displayed in the figure was used only as a lead-in to questions about whether the named friends were members of the respondents' congregations. So, I had to reconstruct the number as follows: Interviewers wrote down the names respondents gave—up to 3 names in 1988 and up to 5 in 1998—and then asked, for each one, "Is [NAME] a member of your congregation?" The variable "frndcon1" codes whether the first named was or was not in the respondent's congregation, whether the respondent did not know the answer, or whether the respondent was not a member of the congregation. The missing-data code "IAP" (inappropriate) presumably indicates that the respondent had not given any names in answer to the lead-in question, "Who are your good friends?" The percentage coded "IAP" mounts from the first to the last name, from variable "frndcon1" to variable "frndcon5." (Another missing data code, NA, not applicable, does not seem a plausible indicator that the respondent gave no name because the number of respondents coded NA remained constant across the frndcon1–5 measures. NA may really indicate a refusal to address the question at all.) I interpret the percentage of respondents (excluding the NA respondents from the base N) who were coded IAP on "frndcon1" as those who said, explicitly or implicitly, that they had no close friends. Those who had a valid code on "frndcon1" but were IAP on "frndcon2" are assumed to have named only one close friend, and so forth through the third name in 1988 and the fifth name in 1998. This yields an estimate of respondents' close friends from zero through three or more in 1988 and from zero to five or more in 1998. I consulted Tom Smith of NORC on these questions (personal communication, November 27, 2009).

Figure 4.4   **Respondents Claiming Fewer Than Three or Six or More Close Friends—Saguaro**

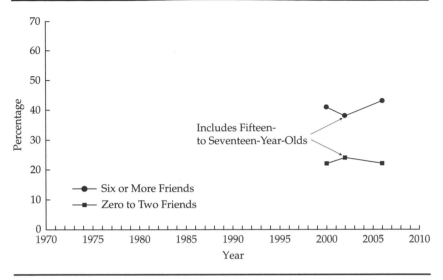

Sources: Social Capital Benchmark Community Surveys, obtained from Roper Center iPoll.
Question: "Now, how about friends? About how many close friends do you have these days? These are people you feel at ease with, can talk to about private matters, or call on for help. Would you say that you have no close friends, one or two, three to five, six to ten, or more than that?"
Note: The 2002 survey includes fifteen- to seventeen-year-olds.

percentage of Americans who reported having no "close friends." Moreover, that percentage remained, despite variations in questions and methods, typically in the single digits.[19]

Turning away from the issue of total friendlessness to the question of many versus few friends, we see no consistent trend on either the high side or the low side; only figure 4.3 shows a change, a drop in the percentage who reported three or more close friends. Other fluctuations in the figures tell no consistent story.[20] In Amato and his colleagues' comparison of married respondents under the age of fifty-five in 1980 and 2000, the number of "close friends" aside from kin declined from a mean estimate of 6.0 to 5.4.[21] In the Wang and Wellman study, the mean number of friends that respondents estimated having went up, from about nine in 2002 to about eleven in 2004, but the median did not.[22] The findings are clearly mixed and do not allow us to infer any time trend.

A couple of studies point to *cohort effects* on American friendships. That is, rather than compare across time periods, we can compare across generations. The paired surveys of married people in the study by Amato and his colleagues yielded a substantial difference: more recently born respondents reported fewer friends.[23] The 2000 versus 2007 study by Wang and Wellman also found that younger respondents reported fewer "off-line" friends, even as each generation seemed to add friends over the seven years of their study.[24] I looked for cohort effects in the GSS polls for figures 4.2 and 4.3. The results were mixed and, in any event, ambiguous, because it is hard to distinguish what is an effect of cohort and what is an effect of age.[25] In short, the cohort issue is open.

(Some readers might expect discussion here of the GSS "important matters" question discussed in chapter 2, but that question is not explicitly about friends, and most confidants are relatives. I include those results in chapter 5, on social support.)

Although counts of Americans' social relations are surprisingly few, many surveys have asked American respondents about how often they see, communicate with, or do activities with people in their social circles. These questions start to get at the substance and perhaps quality of Americans' relationships.

Face-to-Face Contact

I turn next to Americans' contact with nonkin, although the data here are muddied by the practice in many surveys of posing questions that ask about friends and relatives at the same time. In this section, I pool such questions with ones that ask specifically about nonkin relations. I distinguish in-person visiting from conversations by telephone or through other media.

Figure 4.5 shows the 1986 to 2002 difference in the percentage of GSS respondents who picked "at least weekly" in answer to the question "How often do you see or visit with [the friend you feel closest to]?" We see a notable drop from 1986 to 2002, from 65.5 to 54.5 percent.[26]

Figure 4.6 presents the results from two GSS questions about how respondents spent "a social evening": "Would you use this card and tell me which answer comes closest to how often you do the following things? . . . (b) spend a social evening with someone who lives in your neighborhood; (c) spend a social evening with friends who live outside the neighborhood." (Item "a" was the one I discussed earlier about spending a social evening with *relatives*.) The figure displays the trends in the percentages who reported doing so at least weekly. It is worth pausing over these two particular questions.

They are important because, unlike almost any other relevant questions, they have been asked over nearly the entire period covered in this book. And they are important because since at least the 1980s

Figure 4.5   Respondents Who Visit a Best Friend at Least Weekly—GSS

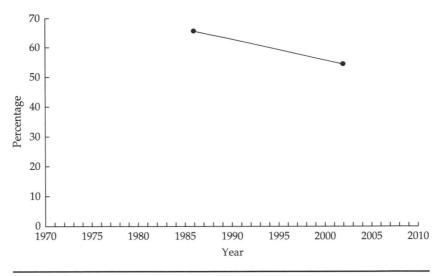

Sources: Author's compilation based on data from GSS items "frivisit," "bstvisit."
Question: "Now thinking of your best friend, or the friend you feel closest to . . . how often
do you see or visit with your friend (the friend you feel closest to)?"
Note: The 1986 version was administered in person, and the 2002 version was part of a
self-administered questionnaire.

social scientists have exhaustively analyzed the time trends in these
two items. Robert Putnam is skeptical about the "friends who live outside the neighborhood" item, saying that it is the only series of friendship questions in several data sets that does not trend downward.[27]
I make such comparisons between data sets later, but for now I note
only that respondents who reported spending more social evenings
with friends also tended to list more nonkin in answer to the "important matters" question[28] and to estimate larger circles of friends in
answer to other questions.[29] As measures of social life go, the "social
evening with friends outside the neighborhood" item is a reasonable
indicator.

Figure 4.6 shows a startlingly flat trend line for the percentage who
reported spending several social evenings a month with friends outside
the neighborhood: 41 percent over the 1970s and 44 percent over the
2000s. (Nor is there any trend at the extremes among those who said that
they never spent such an evening or for those who claimed to have several such evenings a week.[30]) We can also add an earlier point to this
series: when the question was asked in a 1964 survey, 35 percent said

**Figure 4.6   Respondents Who Spend a Social Evening at Least Several
Times a Month with Neighbors or with Friends Outside the
Neighborhood—GSS**

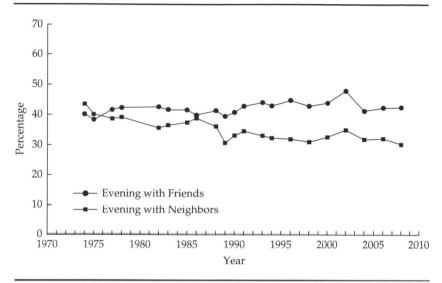

Sources: Author's compilation based on data from GSS items "socommun," "socfrend."
Questions: "Would you use this card and tell me which answer comes closest to how often
you do the following things? . . . (1) Spend a social evening with someone who lives in
your neighborhood." (2) ". . . Spend a social evening with friends who live outside the
neighborhood."

that they spent a social evening with friends at least several times a
month—a figure *lower* than in any subsequent year.[31]

In contrast, the bottom line in figure 4.6 shows a steady decline in the
percentage of GSS respondents who said that they spent at least several
social evenings a month with "someone who lives in your neighborhood": from about 40 percent in the 1970s to about 32 percent in the
2000s. The percentage of GSS respondents who said that they *never* spent
a social evening with neighbors rose a bit, from 24 percent in the 1970s to
29 percent in the 2000s. The 1964 point—at 41 percent, higher than in any
subsequent year—confirms that the slow decline was long-lasting.[32]

(Another item in this GSS series, a question about how often respondents went to a bar or tavern, is not particularly associated with having
social ties. Nonetheless, Putnam and others have used it as a marker of
social life. It shows trivial change, from 18 percent reporting going to a
bar several times a month in the 1970s to 15 percent doing so in the
2000s.[33])

Figure 4.7   Respondents Who Socialize Twice a Week with Friends, Relatives, or Neighbors—Harris, Princeton Associates

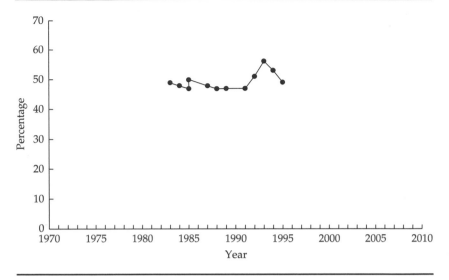

Sources: Author's compilation. Surveys conducted by Louis Harris Associates and later by Princeton Survey Research Associates (PSRA) for *Prevention* magazine, starting with iPoll, USHARRIS.834011.R25, in 1983 and iPoll, USPSRA.92PR10.R14, in 1992.

Question: "About how often do you socialize with close friends, relatives, or neighbors?" Response categories: more than twice a week, twice a week, once a week, two to three times a month, once a month, less than once a month, and never.

Notes: (1) Between 1991 and 1992, the "house" changed from Harris to PSRA. (2) In 1995, PSRA experimented with alternative wording—"About how often do you visit or spend time with close friends, relatives, or neighbors?" The shift from "socialize" to "visit or spend time" raised the percentage of "twice-weekly or more" answers from 53 to 75 percent. The 1995 point in the figure draws from the poll with the original wording ("socialize").

Figure 4.7 reports respondents' answers to a sociability question asked by other survey organizations, one that lumps kin and nonkin together: "About how often do you socialize with close friends, relatives, or neighbors?" From 1983 to 1995, respondents were about as likely—around 50 percent of them—to say that they did so at least monthly.

Similarly, there was no substantive change from 1994 to 2000 in the percentage of respondents who answered "yes" to a Princeton Survey Research Associates (PSRA) question on whether they had visited "with family or friends" the day before the interview; "yes" answers bounced around 66 percent, plus or minus seven points (not shown here).[34] These two series together suggest that there was no net change in socializing or visiting with "friends or family" from 1983 to 2000.

Figure 4.8   Respondents Who Say They Entertained Twelve or More Times a Year and Who Say They Visit Friends a Lot—DDB Needham

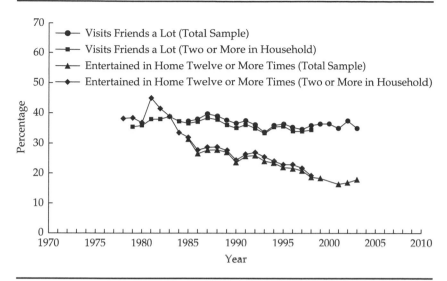

Source: Author's compilation based on data from DDB Needham items "enthome," "visfrd."

Questions: (1) "enthome": Respondents were asked how often they had done various activities in the previous twelve months, including "entertained people in my home," with seven response categories ranging from none, one to four times, up to fifty-two or more times. (2) "visfrd": "I spend a lot of time visiting friends," with six response categories ranging from definitely disagree to definitely agree.

Note: See notes to figure 3.1 for an explanation of the dual lines and discussion of the unusual nature of the sample.

Figure 4.8 shows the results of two questions asked by the DDB Needham organization; for technical reasons I discussed earlier (see figure 3.1 note), answers to each are represented by a pair of overlapping lines. The top pair display the percentage of respondents who agreed with the statement "I spend a lot of time visiting friends." There is effectively no trend.[35] In sharp contrast, the proportion of DDB respondents who said that they "entertained people" in their home at least twelve times in the past year dropped from about two in five to fewer than one in five at the start of the new century.[36] In a related DDB question, the proportion who reported "often"—or even "ever"—giving or attending a "dinner party" in the previous year dropped at least as precipitously.[37] These results suggest that Americans got together with friends in someone's home less often, but overall got together with friends just as often.

Figure 4.9   Respondents Who Went to the Home of Friends and Who Went to a Restaurant in the Previous Week—Roper

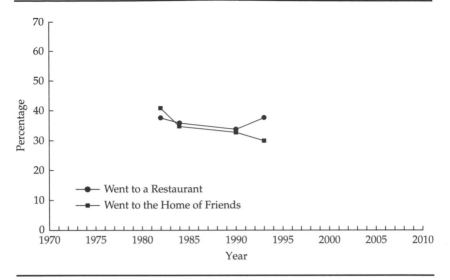

Source: Author's compilation based on data from Roper polls collected by Brady et al. (2000).
Questions: Respondents were asked how often they had gone out for entertainment in the past week. If respondents gave any number more than "once," they were then asked: "Which of these things, if any, have you done during the past week when you went out for entertainment? (1) went to the home of friends for dinner, to play cards, to visit, etc. (2) went to a restaurant for dinner."

Finally, figure 4.9 presents two Roper questions that the organization asked in sequence: "Which of these things, if any, have you done during the past week when you went out for entertainment? (1) Went to the home of friends for dinner, to play cards, to visit, etc. (2) Went to a restaurant for dinner." "Yes" answers to the first question show a clear decline of about ten points from 1982 to 1993, consistent with the DDB trend of less entertaining in the home.[38] I include the second question in the display (and there is no trend), even though that question does not explicitly refer to friends, because it seems to echo an emerging pattern: decline after the 1970s in how often people saw friends in a home setting, but no decline in overall reports of seeing friends. We can assume that a good deal of dining out is done with friends (or family). We can also assume that visits or even simple conversations with neighbors— as in figure 4.6—take place in the home or near the home. Thus, a tentative conclusion might be that meeting friends in home settings declined, but that total meetings did not.[39]

Several published studies provide further evidence as to whether visiting with friends (or friends and relatives) changed over the last few decades for Americans. Notably, Putnam, who reports on trends through the late 1990s in some of the same data discussed here, also finds a decline in "having friends over" between 1976 and 1996. Joseph Veroff, Elizabeth Douvan, and Richard Kulka find a modest but reliable decline in respondents' reports of visiting with friends and relatives between 1957 and 1976.[40]

The same sort of time-budget studies that addressed family time provide another set of data for estimating trends in friends getting together. Measuring time budgets is technically difficult; making comparisons across time when procedures differed from survey to survey is doubly awkward. Nonetheless, such studies show that the time spent by American adults explicitly "visiting" with friends *and* relatives declined from around 1970 into the 2000s, by an average of a few hours a week, or 20 percent per person (and interestingly, it declined more among more-educated Americans). However, Americans' time spent in the company of friends and relatives *while doing something else*—say, going to the movies with friends or supervising a children's playdate with a friend— declined only a small amount.[41] Still, the time-budget studies indicate that Americans spent less face-to-face time with friends and relatives at the end than at the start of the period.

The emerging pattern is consistent in suggesting that Americans "entertained" friends in home settings less often. But most of the evidence also suggests that Americans saw their friends in person about as often in the 2000s as in the 1970s.

Other Contact with Friends (and Others)

With figure 4.10, we turn from *seeing* friends (and relatives) to other modes of being in touch, especially telephone calling. Figure 4.10 complements figure 4.5 and shows essentially no difference between 1986 and 2002 in how often GSS respondents said that they had contact with their "best friends" other than by visiting: in each poll, slightly fewer than two-thirds reported at least weekly contact.[42] Combining this result with the results for visiting a best friend (figure 4.5) suggests a modest shift from visiting to calling. In net, the percentage of GSS respondents who either visited with or called their best friends at least weekly was 77 percent in 1986 and 73 percent in 2002—a borderline change.

Figure 4.11 displays answers to a follow-up question that Princeton Survey Research Associates posed after asking respondents whether they had visited with family or friends the day before. As with visiting, there was essentially no trend between 1994 and 2004 in the percentage

Figure 4.10   Respondents in Contact with Best Friend at Least Weekly—GSS

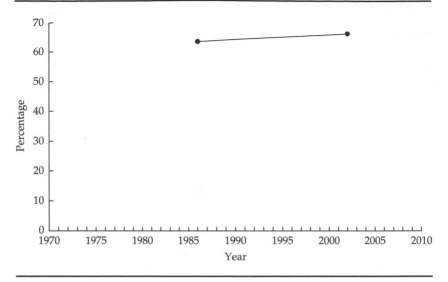

Sources: Author's compilation based on data from GSS items "fricall," "bstcall."
Questions: 1986: "And how often do you have any other contact with this [best] friend besides visiting, either by telephone or letter? [2002: '. . . either by telephone, letter, fax, or email?'].
Note: The 1986 version was administered in person, and the 2002 version was part of a self-administered questionnaire.

of respondents who said that they had called friends or relatives the day before.[43]

Figure 4.12 covers an earlier part of the period, 1975 through 1992, and displays responses to Roper's question, "Thinking of the mail you send out, aside from bills and things like that, about how many personal letters have you written to friends or relatives in the past month?" followed by "And how many phone calls to friends and relatives over one hundred miles away have you made in the past month?" While reported rates of letter-writing remained essentially flat—about 30 percent had written three or more times—reported long-distance calls to friends or relatives increased substantially after 1984 (coinciding with a steep drop in the cost of long-distance calling), from under 40 percent saying that they made three such calls a month to nearly 60 percent doing so.[44] To these two parallel Roper questions, I added a third. Interviewers asked respondents to look at a list of activities and to call off the ones they had "done in the last week, either at home or at work," including "made a long-distance phone call (more than one hundred miles) at home or work." The trend for call-

Figure 4.11   Respondents Who Called a Friend or Relative the Day Before—PSRA

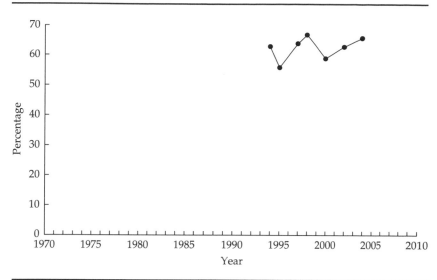

Source: Author's compilation based on data from surveys conducted by PSRA for the Times Mirror Company in 1994 and 1995 and for Pew Research Center for the People and the Press afterwards. Accessed through iPoll, USPSRA.052494.R11G to USPSRA.060804. R20HF1.
Questions: "Yesterday did you: . . . call a friend or relative just to talk?"
Notes: (1) In 2001 respondents to the 2000 survey were reinterviewed; 61 percent said "yes," but that data point is not included in the figure. (2) Notes to the 1998 survey specifically say that respondents interviewed on Sunday were asked about Friday. It is not clear if similar instructions were given in other years. (3) In 1997, PSRA conducted two waves, one being a special, "rigorous" survey that raised response rates from 42 to 71 percent. The result for the "standard" survey is shown in the figure; the result for the "rigorous" survey was one point higher.

ing based on this item (shown by the line with diamonds) is also upward, although not as steeply or consistently.[45] The calling question with the steeper trend specifically refers to relatives and friends, but it is also less exact and perhaps more prone to exaggeration.

One more series on calling can be added to our canvass (not shown). The 1990 to 1992 and 2001 to 2003 National Comorbidity Studies mentioned earlier asked, "How often do you talk on the phone or get together with friends?" In both the earlier period and the later one, 56 percent of the eighteen- to fifty-four-year-old sample said "at least a few times a week" or "almost every day."[46]

These questions about contact are vague; people could be calling to have conversations about important matters or just to say hello. The

Figure 4.12   Respondents Who Called or Wrote Distant Friends or Relatives Three or More Times in Previous Month (and Who Called Long-Distance Last Week to Anyone)—Roper

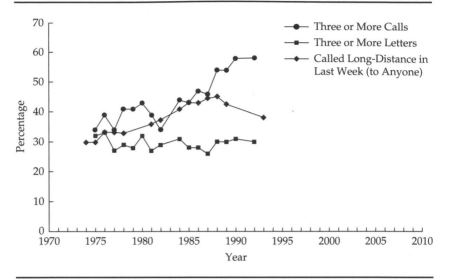

Source: Author's compilation based on data from polls as reported in Roper Reports and archived at iPoll service; data set compiled by Brady et al. (2000).
Questions: (1) "And how many phone calls to friends and relatives over one hundred miles away have you made in the past month?" (2) "Thinking of the mail you send out, aside from bills and things like that, about how many personal letters have you written to friends or relatives in the past month?" (3) "Would you read down that list and call off each one you personally have done in the last week, either at home or at work? . . . made a long-distance phone call (more than one hundred miles) at home or work."

American National Election Survey allows us to focus on one particular kind of conversation with friends and relatives—those specifically about politics. Admittedly, this is a limited topic for personal relationships. And whether people have such conversations is influenced by the political climate—say, by whether it is the year of a presidential election. Nonetheless, the ANES measures have the advantage of covering many years and also of providing some substance to "talk." (When respondents are asked open-ended questions about what they talk about, the topics that come to their minds vary and can be idiosyncratic.[47]) The top line in figure 4.13 shows the percentage of respondents who said "yes" to "Do you ever discuss politics with your family or friends?" The second line from the top displays the percentage—among those who said that, yes, they did discuss politics—of those who then said that they had done so on at least three days in the previous week. Both lines show moderate upward trends in discussing politics, even setting aside the

Figure 4.13   Respondents Who Discussed Politics—ANES and Roper

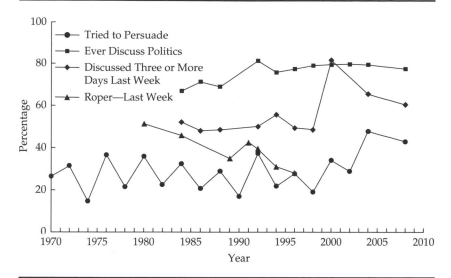

Sources: Author's compilation. ANES analyzed online via SDA, University of California–Berkeley: Roper Reports, Brady et al. (2000), plus the 1996 point as reported by Putnam (2000, 448, note 13).
Questions: (1) ANES "vcf0731": "Do you ever discuss politics with your family or friends?" (asked 1984 through 2008) (2) ANES "vcf0733": "How many days in the past week did you talk about politics with your family or friends?" (1984 through 2000, 2004, and 2008; see note below about 2002) (3) ANES "vcf0717": "During the campaign, did you talk to any people and try to show them why they should vote for [1984 and later: 'or against'] one of the parties or candidates?" (1952 through 2008) (4) Roper: "PAPOLS": "Would you read down that list and call off each one you personally have done in the last week, either at home or at work? . . . discussed politics with someone."
Notes: (1) All ANES analyses used weight = "vcf0009A" (although weighting variations made only minute differences). (2) For "vcf0733", the online data show a zero score—talked no days in past week—for 100 percent of the respondents in 2002. I treated that year as missing data.

anomaly of the 2000 election. (This question was asked in the post-election part of the ANES, and we can presume that the 2000 surge in talking had to do with interest in the Bush-Gore deadlock after election day. A remarkable 40 percent reported discussing politics every day of the week during that month, about triple the rates of the prior and following presidential elections.) And the upward trends are robust after controlling for other attributes—including the respondents' interest in politics.[48]

The lowest, sawtooth line tracks respondents' affirmative answers to the question of whether they tried to talk others into voting their way. That up-and-down pattern reflects differences between presidential and off-year elections. (The ANES asked this question starting in 1952; the percentage of affirmative answers in the 1950s and 1960s ran slightly *below* those from 1970 on.) And if we statistically control for respondents' level of general political engagement, the slight upward trend in reported persuasion persists.[49]

Figure 4.13, finally, also displays a line of data from the Roper surveys: the percentage of respondents who "called off" from a list of activities that they had "discussed politics with someone" in the last week. These results roughly parallel the ANES findings in the comparable years until 1992: after 1992 the Roper data suggest a continuing decline, while the ANES data do not. The reason for the contradiction is unclear.[50] Most scholars would assume that the ANES data are the more reliable.[51] We should conclude that Americans reported talking *more* to friends and relatives about politics in the 2000s than in the 1970s (and even before). Perhaps, as has been suggested,[52] it has become more culturally permissible to discuss politics in polite company. But given that considerable research has described Americans as withdrawing from politics after the mid-1960s—voting less, trusting government less, knowing less about politics, and so on—finding that Americans reported talking politics with friends and family more, even lobbying them more, seems to suggest that it is the *talking* that went up rather than the *politics*.[53]

Putting together the items, Americans seemed to have been talking more with friends—both physically and virtually—over the last few decades.

Conclusions

Agglomerating these surveys and assuming that each gives us a partial view of what happened suggests that American adults of the late 2000s, compared to American adults of the early 1970s:

- Were no more and no less likely to be friendless (a finding that, of course, challenges the conventional wisdom—at least outside of network studies—but that is what the weight of the data clearly show)

- Had roughly the same median number of friends, although recent cohorts may not have been as likely to have *many* friends

- Entertained friends and neighbors in their homes less often

- Probably saw friends in person as often or less; the data are mixed

- Were otherwise in touch with their friends as often as adults of the earlier period, or, probably, more often

For all the "lonely, friendless American" chatter in the media, the evidence suggests that friendship was as healthy in America in the 2000s as in the 1970s—although dinner parties and the like were not.

Chapter 5

Counting on People

THIS CHAPTER turns from Americans' descriptions of their bonds with family and friends to their expectations for getting help from those people. Friends and relatives assist one another practically by, for example, moving furniture, providing job tips, or lending money; socially by doing things like going to the movies together, playing tennis, or making introductions to potential friends; and psychologically by discussing personal problems, boosting each other when they feel "down," or just "being there" for each other. Too often, as noted in chapter 1, discussions of "social support" fail to recognize that friends and relatives also hinder one another: they demand practical assistance, interfere with other social relationships, and create anxiety. The difficulty that researchers have had in confirming a strong connection between social ties and psychological benefits (discussed in chapter 2) may result in part from these conflicting patterns. In three national surveys, each about thirty years apart, Americans who said that they had at some time felt the onset of a possible "nervous breakdown" were asked what led to that feeling. Especially in recent years, the major reason offered by respondents was something about their relationships, notably their marital or romantic relationships (more on these studies later).[1] Indeed, we do not need a psychiatrist to tell us that the most important relationships in people's lives bring them both joy and tribulation.

The question here is whether and how Americans' evaluations of their personal support changed between 1970 and 2010. Unfortunately, trend data on support are even rarer and more fragmentary than those on the number of friends and relatives that people say they have. And most of the trend data concern emotional or psychological support rather than more mundane practical help. Nonetheless, we can discern some patterns.

Family

One reason the kin-versus-nonkin distinction matters so much is precisely the question of support. Home—that is, family—is "where they have to take you in." The norms and practice of helping relatives, at least close ones, are strong and continuing (even) in the United States. The World Values Survey (WVS) has repeatedly used a pair of questions testing respondents' commitment to family obligations. One question asked:

> With which of these two statements do you tend to agree? (A) Regardless of what the qualities and faults of one's parents are, one must always love and respect them; (B) One does not have the duty to respect and love parents who have not earned it by their behavior and attitudes.

Between 1982 and 1999, with trivial change, about 75 percent of Americans picked the first answer—the "one must always love and respect them" option. Americans answered that way considerably less often than did respondents in countries like Egypt and India, but considerably more often than did respondents in countries like Britain and Sweden. (In 1999 most Swedes picked the "does not have the duty" option). The companion WVS question asked:

> Which of the following statements best describes your views about parents' responsibilities to their children? (A) Parents' duty is to do their best for their children even at the expense of their own well-being; (B) Parents have a life of their own and should not be asked to sacrifice their own well-being for the sake of their children.

The percentage of American respondents saying that "parents' duty is to do their best for their children even at the expense of their own well-being" rose from 72 percent in 1982 to 86 percent in 1999, putting them among Indians and Egyptians on this issue.[2]

A GSS item (which I discuss further in the next chapter) also taps a sense of family duty: "As you know, many older people share a home with their grown children. Do you think this is generally a good idea or a bad idea?" In the 1970s, 35 percent said that it was a good idea; in the 2000s, 50 percent gave this answer.[3] Americans' relatively high sense of family obligations may surprise observers who describe American culture as individualistic, but it is a persistent trait.[4]

American parents and adult children give one another help at high rates, studies show, whether motivated by affection (more commonly among daughters) or duty (more commonly among sons). The overriding determinant of how much financial and personal help elderly parents and adult children provide each other, aside from how much they can afford to give, is the other person's need—which suggests that people feel obligations to help. A 2005 survey found that at least three-quarters of young adults got some financial help from their parents, that over half received more than $1,000 a year, and that aging parents gave their adult children about 10 percent of their own income. In a 2007 survey, a large majority of American adults reported giving either financial or personal assistance to a parent or said that they expected to do so.[5] It would be helpful to have over-time reports on such intergenerational exchanges, but it appears that we do not have reliable trend data.[6] One reviewer of the literature suggests that the smaller family sizes and the delay in marriage in recent decades may have increased the volume of parent-child mutual support.[7]

Reports of Practical Support

The GSS provides two snapshots of how confident Americans were in getting practical help from family and friends, one for 1986 and the other for 2002. Although asked slightly differently in the two years, each time the GSS interviewer provided respondents with a printed questionnaire that included questions about who would help them if they were sick and who would help them if they needed money. (There was also a question about personal advice, which I discuss later.) The illness question read:

> Suppose you had the flu and you had to stay in bed for a few days and needed help around the home, with shopping and such [2002: "with shopping, and so on"]. . . . Who would you turn to first for help? . . . Who would you turn to second?

Following each probe came a list: "spouse, mother, father, daughter," and so on, through "coworker, nurse, paid help, other," and, explicitly, "no one." Extremely few respondents checked "no one": 2 percent in each year. Similarly, only 3 and 4 percent in 1986 and 2002, respectively, provided only one name.

Figure 5.1 shows some more results from this question. I divided the sample into the unmarried and the married because married respondents overwhelmingly favored their spouse as a caretaker. The bottom pair of lines displays the percentage of respondents who checked off fewer than two personal helpers. (Some respondents marked "nurse" or "paid help," but unless they checked "friend," "neighbor," "coworker," or "family" *both* first and second, they are coded as having fewer than two personal helpers.[8]) We see negligible differences—there was essentially no change in this indicator of having weak social support. Something else, however, did seem to change. As the top lines show, there was a shift toward checking off relatives. However, I would caution against over-interpreting the trend: it may be the result of wording changes between the 1986 and 2002 versions. The 2002 questionnaire provided a richer list of relatives.[9] The bottom lines are the bottom line: little change between 1986 and 2002 in Americans' expectations of personal support if they got sick.[10]

Figure 5.1   Respondents with Fewer than Two Personal Helpers and Those with Relatives As Helpers If Sick—GSS

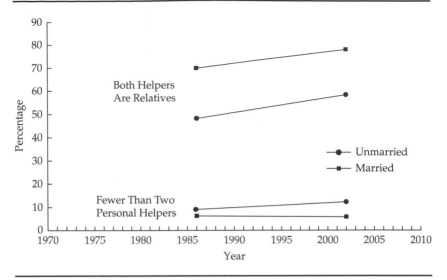

Source: Author's compilation based on data from GSS items "sick1," "sick2," "sick1a," "sick2a."

Questions: 1986: "Suppose you had the flu and you had to stay in bed for a few days and needed help around the home, with shopping and such. (a) Who would you turn to first for help? (b) Who would you turn to second?" 2002: "Now we would like to ask you how you would get help in situations that anyone could find herself or himself in. First, suppose you had the flu and had to stay in bed for a few days and needed help around the house, with shopping and so on. (a) Who would you turn to first for help? (b) Who would you turn to second?" The 1986 response categories were "spouse, mother, father, daughter, son, sister, brother, other relative, closest friend, other friend, neighbor, coworker, clergy, family doctor, professional counselor, no one" (and "no answer"). The 2002 response categories were "husband-wife-partner, mother, father, daughter, son, sister, brother, other blood relative, other in-law relative, close friend, neighbor, someone you work with, priest or member of the clergy, family doctor, a psychologist or other professional counselor, a self-help group, someone else, no one" (and "don't know" and "no answer").

Notes: (1) I recoded the roughly three dozen "no answers" that had been coded missing data to "no help," assuming that respondents who did not answer included many who would have had answered that they lacked help if pressed. That decision had negligible effect on the trend. (2) In both years, the questions appeared on a self-administered questionnaire. (3) Note that the 2002 version included a longer list of relatives and also replaced "spouse" as an option with "husband-wife-partner." Note also that in 2002, but not in 1986, some respondents named "husband-wife-partner" twice, which I took to mean a current spouse and an ex-spouse. (4) The contexts of the questions differed. The 1986 help questions—if sick, if needed money, if "down"—were part of a longer set of such questions; in 2002 they stood alone. In 2002 the three help topics followed a long battery of questions asking about how often respondents got together with and contacted various relatives and friends, and also questions about organizational memberships.

The GSS asked a parallel question about money in the same years: "Suppose you needed to borrow a large sum of money. . . . Who would you turn to first [second] for help?" Unfortunately, an oddity in the results makes it hard to compare across the years, as I did with the flu question: in 1986 about one in two respondents checked "bank/credit union/ financial institution/savings and loan" first or second; in 2002 only about one in ten checked "a bank or credit union" or "a private money lender" first or second. It is unclear whether this shift reflects a real change in borrowing practices over the sixteen years or some methodological artifact, which is what I suspect.[11] The answers covering professional lenders account for the fact that 5 percent of the 1986 respondents but 11 percent of the 2002 respondents checked "no one" or did not answer the question. We can retrieve some use of the item by asking about *personal* sources of loans. Eighty percent of respondents in 1986 and 79 percent in 2002 checked a personal connection—almost always a relative—as at least one source of a loan.[12] At best, this is a crude question, but it suggests, again, that no change occurred over the period in how many Americans were stuck without personal help.

Surprisingly, this is all I have found about receiving practical help in repeated national surveys.[13] There is, on the other hand, more trend data on respondents' reports of psychological or emotional support.

Reports of Emotional Support

Along with the flu and money questions, the GSS in 1986 and 2002 asked, "Now suppose you feel just a bit down or depressed, and you want to talk about it. . . . Who would you turn to first [second] for help?" Response categories were the same: "spouse," "mother," on through "counselor," "someone else," or "no one." Virtually everyone checked some kind of relative or friend. Two percent and 3 percent in 1986 and 2002, respectively, checked "no one" or left both options unanswered; 6 percent and 8 percent checked fewer than two kinds of relations. Figure 5.2 shows, in the lower two lines, the percentage of respondents each year—separately for the married and the unmarried—who checked fewer than two personal sources of help, be they relative or friend. There is a drop of a few points between 1986 and 2002, which seems largely the result of far fewer respondents checking "clergy" (and that may be a real change or an effect of the wording).[14] As in the case of the flu question, the percentage who checked relatives both first and second rose a sizable amount. Again, this may be a real change, a methodological artifact, or perhaps a bit of both.[15] The take-away message, in any case, is that few Americans failed to nominate a personal friend or relative who would help them deal with depression, and that percentage did not change over the sixteen years.[16]

Figure 5.2   Respondents with Fewer Than Two Personal Helpers and Those with Two Relatives As Helpers If Feeling Down—GSS

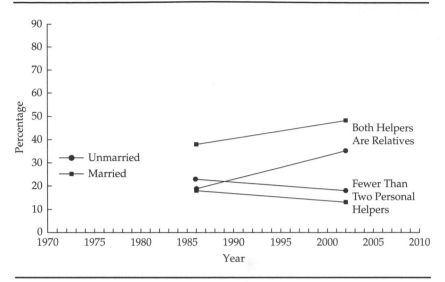

Source: Author's compilation based on data from GSS items "down1," "down2," "down1a," "down2a."
Question: "Now suppose you feel just a bit down or depressed, and you wanted to talk about it. . . . Who would you turn to first [second] for help?" For the response categories, see figure 5.1.
Note: See figure 5.1.

We have two relatively similar points in time from the National Comorbidity Studies cited earlier—the large-scale national health survey conducted from 1990 to 1992 and then replicated in 2001 to 2003. One set of questions dealt specifically with the support—and demands—that respondents reported receiving from their spouses. Table 5.1 displays the results specifically of the support items. (Only eighteen- to fifty-four-year-olds are covered because the first wave did not interview people over fifty-four.)

The table shows, in the statistics for answers to the first four questions, either no changes or changes in a positive direction over the decade. The last row shows results from an additional question: Did respondents regularly turn to their spouse with their worries? Again, no change.[17]

The same pair of surveys also contains a battery of questions about support and emotional engagement with friends and relatives, displayed in table 5.2. One item presents a notable decline in perceived supportiveness: fewer respondents in 2001 to 2003 said that they could rely on their

Table 5.1   Responses to Spouse Support Questions—National
Comorbidity Studies, Eighteen- to Fifty-Four-Year-Olds

	1990 to 1992	2001 to 2003
1) Respondents answering "a lot" to the question[a]: "How much . . .		
. . . does your (husband/wife/partner) really care about you?"	93%	94%
. . . does (he/she) understand the way you feel about things?"	60	82
. . . can you rely on (him/her) for help if you have a serious problem?"	89	90
. . . can you open up to (him/her) if you need to talk about your worries?"	72	77
2) Respondents answering "always" or "most of the time" to the question[b]: "When you have a problem or worry, how often do you let your (husband/wife/partner) know about it?"	70	69

Source: Author's compilation. National Comorbidity Survey: Baseline (NCS-1), 1990–1992, obtained from University of Michigan, Inter-University Consortium for Political and Social Research (ICPSR) study 6693; National Comorbidity Survey Replication (NCS-R), 2001–2003, ICPSR study 189.

Notes: The weights are P2WTV3 for 1990 to 1992 and NCSRWTLG for 2001 to 2003, although different weights seem to make little difference. The sample is restricted to eighteen- to fifty-four-year-olds to make the two surveys comparable. The (weighted) sample sizes for these questions are about 3,500 for wave 1 and about 1,000 for wave 2 (although the numbers of actual cases is over 5,000). It appears that the smaller number of respondents in the second survey was a result of subselection—apparently at random—for a "couples sample" (ICPSR, personal correspondence, December 2009 to January 2010). The variables that match up are, from the 1990 to 1992 study, "v201," "v202," "v204," "v205," "v207," "v210," "v211," and "v212," and correspondingly from the 2001 to 2003 study, "MR41_1A" through "MR41_1D" and "MR41_2A" through "MR41_2D." (Several questions in this realm were asked only in the first survey.)
[a] The response categories were: "a lot," "some," "a little," and "not at all."
[b] The response categories were: "always," "most of the time," "sometimes," "rarely," and "never."

relatives "a lot"; the percentage who said that they could rely on them only a little or "not at all" rose from 11 percent a decade earlier to 18 percent. However, the wording of this question changed, probably critically: the 1990 to 1992 version asked about relatives; the 2001 to 2003 version asked about relatives "who do not live with you." Otherwise, the results show little change in how much support respondents expected.

To these data we can add some additional survey results that shed light on the emotional support question. First, the Louis Harris organization twice asked the same question: "Now, I'd like to read you some more

Table 5.2   Responses to Relatives and Friends Support Questions—
National Comorbidity Studies, Eighteen- to Fifty-Four-Year-Olds

	1990 to 1992	2001 to 2003
Support from relatives		
Respondents answering "a lot" to the question[a]: "(Not counting your husband/wife/partner), how much . . .		
. . . can you rely on [1990 to 1992: 'your relatives'; 2001 to 2003: 'relatives who do not live with you'] for help if you have a serious problem?"	74%	62%
. . . can you open up to [1990 to 1992: 'them'; 2001 to 2003: 'relatives who do not live with you'] if you need to talk about your worries?"	45	46
Support from friends		
Respondents answering "a lot" to the question[a]: "How much . . .		
. . . can you rely on [1990 to 1992: 'them'; 2001 to 2003: 'your friends'] if you have a serious problem?"	51	48
. . . can you open up to [1990 to 1992: 'them'; 2001 to 2003: 'your friends'] if you need to talk about your worries?"	47	49

Source: Author's compilation. National Comorbidity Survey: Baseline (NCS-1), 1990–1992, obtained from University of Michigan, Inter-University Consortium for Political and Social Research (ICPSR) study 6693; National Comorbidity Survey Replication (NCS-R), 2001–2003, ICPSR study 189.
Notes: For details see notes to table 5.1, with the variation that the weighted n for 1990 to 1992 is about 5,300 and for 2001 to 2003 about 5,700. The variables used from the 2001 to 2003 survey are numbers "SN2" through "SN10"; they correspond to these variables in the 1990 to 1992 survey: "v217," "v218," "v220," "v222," "v230," "v231," "v233," "v235."
[a] The response categories were: "a lot," "some," "a little," and "not at all."

statements. Please say for each one if it expresses the way you yourself feel, or not . . . 'I have someone I can share my personal problems with when I need to.' " In both 1978 and 1990, 7 percent of respondents said that they did not have such a confidant or that they were "not sure."[18]

Second, in 1950, twenty years before the period we are focused on, Gallup asked respondents, "When you have personal problems, do you like to discuss them with anyone to help clear them up, or not?" At that time, 37 percent—*over one-third*—said "no" or "don't know." About forty years later, Gallup asked a few related questions, although none of them explicitly included a "no" answer, as the 1950 probe had. A 1989 question asked, "When you have a serious personal problem, who do you turn to for advice, *other* than your husband/wife?" and 13 percent answered "don't know." In 1990 Gallup asked, "Who do you usually talk to first when you have a personal problem . . . [read and rotate:] a friend, your husband or wife, your parents, your children, or other family members?" Seven percent volunteered "no one" or "don't know." Also in 1990, Gallup asked respondents how many friends (who were *not* relatives) they had and later asked, "How often do you and your friends . . . turn to each other with personal problems . . . very often, somewhat often, not too often, or never?" Twelve percent said that either they had no nonrelative friends or that their friends never turned to each other with personal problems.[19] We can make only a crude comparison between these recent numbers on the percentage who report discussing personal problems and the 37 percent who in 1950 said that they did not like to discuss personal problems, but the figures certainly lean against the suggestion that Americans felt a growing sense of isolation over the last forty (or even sixty) years.

Third, the GSS provides us with a few onetime estimates of twenty-first-century respondents' access to confidants. We cannot discern any trends with these items, but they are suggestive in this way: if in recent years the percentage of respondents reporting that they had no confidants is near zero, it would be improbable that the proportion of such people grew substantially over the previous forty years.

1. The GSS asked a question in 2002 (mentioned in chapter 4): "Not counting people at work or family at home, about how many other friends or relatives do you keep in contact with at least once a year?" One percent said "none." Interviewers asked the remaining 99 percent, "Of these friends and relatives, about how many would you say you feel really close to, that is, close enough to discuss personal or important problems with?" Of these respondents, 4 percent said "no one," for a total in 2002 of 5 percent who said that they had no one— *besides* coworkers and immediate family—to "discuss personal or important problems with."[20] Presumably, had the question allowed respondents to consider coworkers and family, the percentage who said "no one" would have been virtually nil.

2. In 2006 the GSS asked a series of questions to get at intergroup trust with this introduction: "Now I'm going to ask you some questions about people that [*sic*] you trust, for example, good friends, people you discuss important matters with, or trust for advice, or trust with money." Interviewers then asked about 650 of the respondents, randomly chosen, "How many [of the people you trust] are Asian or Asian American . . . black or African American . . . Hispanic . . .

white?" (The GSS asked other subsets of respondents how many of the people they trusted were electricians or lawyers or how many were named Brenda or José, and so on.) Adding up the number of trusted people across the four ethno-racial groups is a pretty good estimate of how many people in total were trusted by the respondents. Four percent of the respondents said that there was no one whom they trusted who was Asian, black, Hispanic, or white. (Three percent reported one person over all four ethnic categories, and 10 percent reported a total of two trustworthy people.)[21] Thus, in 2006, about 4 percent of GSS respondents said that they lacked anyone to "discuss important matters with, or trust for advice."

3. In both 2002 and 2004, the GSS asked respondents whether they counseled someone *else:* "During the past twelve months, how often have you done any of the following things for people you know personally, such as relatives, friends, neighbors, or other acquaintances? . . . Spent time talking with someone who was a bit down or depressed." Six percent reported "not at all," and 56 percent said that they did it at least once a month. Although there is no reason to assume that the rate of counseling and the rate of being counseled should be symmetric—some people specialize in providing shoulders to cry on—this result suggests that the percentage of people in 2002 to 2004 who were so isolated that they had not provided a shoulder in a year to anyone was very small, about 6 percent.[22]

We cannot conclude from these three GSS items asked since 2000 whether the total volume of psychological support that Americans felt they could count on had grown or shrunk, because the questions were not asked earlier. But they do point toward this conclusion: about 5 percent of twenty-first-century Americans said that they had no such ties. That percentage is unlikely, then, to have been much lower in the previous decades.

Keeping in mind all these data showing that a very low percentage of Americans said in various ways that they had no one to provide emotional support and showing no trends in that percentage, we can look again at the 1985, 1987, and 2004 GSS "important matters" question. This is the question that elicited names of people with whom the respondent discussed important matters in the previous six months. The results are shown in figure 5.3. In 2004, 23 percent of respondents presumably gave no names in answer to that question, a threefold increase from 8 percent in 1985. I have argued that the 23 percent must be the result of a major error; McPherson and his co-authors agree that the 23 percent is to some extent inflated, but contend that there was still a large increase in the

Figure 5.3   Respondents Who Give Three or More Names or Give No
Names to "Important Matters" Question—GSS

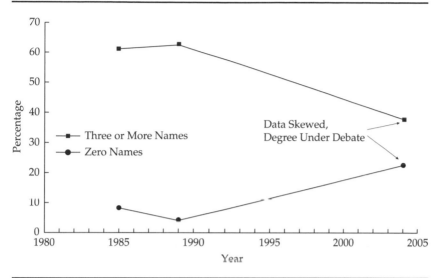

Source: Author's compilation based on data from GSS item "numgiven."
Question: "From time to time, most people discuss important matters with other people. Looking back over the last six months, who are the people with whom you discussed matters important to you?" Interviewers record up to five names (three in 1987).
Notes: (1) As discussed in text, the 2004 points are in error, exaggerating isolation; how much is under dispute. McPherson, Smith-Lovin, and Brashears (2006, 2009) agree that the zero estimate of 23 percent is too high, but contend that the population value is higher than my estimate (Fischer 2009) of about 10 percent. (2) The figure accounts for forty-one originally miscoded cases in 2004. (3) In 1985 and 2004, interviewers were supposed to encourage respondents to provide at least five names, and in 1987 at least three.

percentage of Americans who had discussed important matters with no one—that is, who lacked confidants.[23] Whatever the outcome of the debate over the 2004 GSS, it is clear that the 23 percent is *anomalous*. No other contemporary data point measuring confidants is anywhere close to that level, and no other data set shows a trend anything like it.

Just as there are few over-time data sets that allow us to answer the question of whether Americans' social support has changed (or reports of their social support), there is little published research on time trends. Replications in 1976 and 1996 of a 1957 national mental health survey provided a nearly half-century comparison of Americans' answers to the question of whether they had ever felt that they were going to have a nervous breakdown and, if so, how they had dealt with it. The percentage who reported turning to friends and family rose from 6 percent in

1957 to 12 percent in 1976 and to 28 percent in 1996. (The percentage who mentioned mental health professionals also rose rapidly, while the percentage who said that they turned to a medical doctor fell greatly.)[24] That fragment of research, put together with almost all the data gathered in this section, would suggest no decrease—maybe even an increase—in Americans' perceptions that they have people to draw on in times of emotional or psychological need.

Reports of Tribulation

As pointed out before, the same people who help us are often the same people who hurt us—or at least they can be demanding. We can think of such demands as negative entries on the social support ledger. The surveys of the National Comorbidity Studies specifically asked about that aspect of social relationships. Table 5.3 presents the 1990 to 1992 and 2001 to 2003 results for questions asking about stresses and demands. We see that the level of spousal demands and stress that respondents described stayed constant or declined between the two time periods. And the bottom part of table 5.3 shows that respondents in the later period reported slightly fewer demands and arguments from relatives and friends. These data indicate no real change in how put upon by spouses and friends Americans felt.

The GSS provides a comparison between 1991 and 2004, roughly the same period, in respondents' reports of having "serious" trouble with spouses, children, or friends. The question asked:

"What about family and personal relationships? During the last year, did you . . . (1) Have serious trouble with your husband/wife/partner; (2) Separate from your husband/wife/partner; (3) Break up with a steady boyfriend/girlfriend or fiancé(e); (4) Have serious trouble with a child; (5) Have serious trouble with a close friend?"[25]

The results are complex but suggest that there was specifically an increase in romantic breakups, but not other troubles. Only a small percentage in each year reported "serious trouble with [their] husband/wife/partner" *other than* actually breaking up—no change.[26]

Figure 5.4 focuses on respondents who *did* report a breakup with or a separation from a spouse, partner, or boyfriend (girlfriend) in the previous year. Between 1991 and 2004, many more of the formerly married (divorced, separated, or widowed), and especially the never-married, reported such breakups.[27] This was an era when actual annual divorce rates declined,[28] so figure 5.4 cannot be reflecting legal dissolutions. In all likelihood, it reflects what has been called the "expansion of cohabitation.

Table 5.3   Responses to Demands and Stress Questions—National
Comorbidity Studies, Eighteen- to Fifty-Four-Year-Olds

	1990 to 1992	2001 to 2003
Spouses		
Respondents answering "often" or "sometimes" to the question[a]: "Does your (husband/wife/partner) . . .		
. . . make too many demands on you?"	45%	29%
. . . criticize you?"	28	22
. . . let you down when you are counting on (him/her)?"	17	15
. . . get on your nerves?"	47	46
Friends		
Respondents answering "rarely" or "never" to the question[a]: "How often . . .		
. . . do your friends make too many demands on you?"	25	14
. . . do [1990 to 1992: 'they'; 2001 to 2003: 'your friends'] argue with you?"	18	11

Source: National Comorbidity Survey: Baseline (NCS-1), 1990–1992, obtained from University of Michigan, Inter-University Consortium for Political and Social Research (ICPSR) study 6693; National Comorbidity Survey Replication (NCS-R), 2001–2003, ICPSR study 189.
[a]The response categories were: "often," "sometimes," "rarely," and "never."

As cohabitation becomes increasingly accepted, cohabitations may include a greater proportion of couples with less serious commitments . . . leading to . . . higher dissolution rates"[29]—and probably greater turnover in dating relationships as well. Recall that the delay of marriage means that today's "emerging adults" have more time in the dating period of their lives.

The GSS also asked respondents whether they had had "serious trouble with a close friend" in the past year. Overall, 5 percent said "yes" in 1991 and 6 percent said "yes" in 2004—no change. However, close inspection shows one particular subgroup for which time made a difference: those who had *also* said "yes" to the previous question asking whether they had broken up "with a steady boyfriend/girlfriend or fiancé(e)"—45 respondents in 1991 and 109 respondents in 2004 (see figure 5.5). The 2004 respondents who had reported a breakup in part 2 of the GSS question were much more likely than the 1991 respondents who had reported a breakup to also report trouble with "a close friend" in part 4 of the question.[30] If we assume that for many in this particular group the "close friend" they said they had trouble with was the same "boyfriend/girlfriend or fiancé(e)" they had broken up with, then we are

Figure 5.4   Respondents Who Reported a Breakup with a Spouse or Partner in the Past Year, by Marital Status—GSS

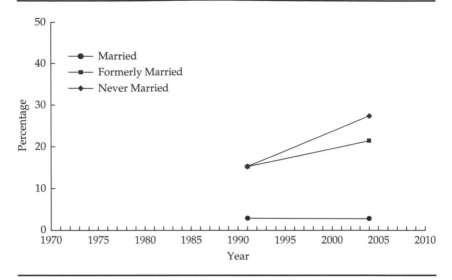

Source: Author's compilation based on data from GSS items "famper1" through "famper3."

Questions: "What about family and personal relationships? During the last year, did you . . . (1) Have serious trouble with your husband/wife/partner; (2) Separate from your husband/wife/partner; (3) Break up with a steady boyfriend/girlfriend or fiancé(e)?"

Notes: (1) The variable in figure 5.4 measures whether respondents reported a breakup in answer to questions "famper2" or "famper3," whether or not they reported trouble in "famper1." (2) In 2004 respondents were also asked specifically whether they had gotten a divorce ("famper6"), but that had not been asked in 1991. In 2004, 60 percent of those who reported a breakup in "famper6" had also reported one in "famper2" or "famper3."

brought back to the rise in dating, cohabitation, and romantic turnovers. (Perhaps the trouble respondents had was with different friends, not the departed boyfriend or girlfriend, but the friendships were stressed by the romantic breakup.) The emerging pattern in the "serious trouble" questions is that there was overall no increase in partner or friendship problems, but there were more breakups of romantic, nonmarital ties.

Finally, the GSS also asked about "serious trouble" with a child (see figure 5.6). On the whole, the 1991 versus 2004 difference is not statistically significant, but there was again one subgroup for whom 2004 reports of trouble were slightly more common than they had been among 1991 reports—parents who had no children under age twenty-five living with them. In 2004, 5 percent of these respondents complained about serious trouble with a child—probably about an adult child living elsewhere— compared to 2 percent in 1991.[31] We know nothing else about these ties, so I can only speculate that in 2004 parents experienced more difficulty

Figure 5.5   Respondents Who Reported Serious Trouble with a Close Friend in the Past Year, by Whether Respondent Broke Up with Boyfriend/Girlfriend in the Past Year—GSS

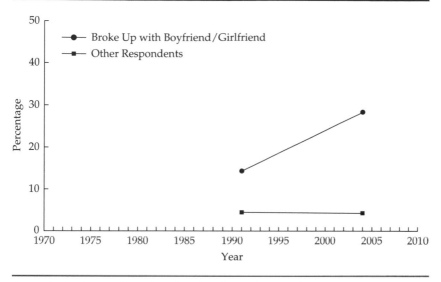

Source: Author's compilation based on data from GSS item "famper5."
Questions: "What about family and personal relationships? During the last year, did you
. . . have serious trouble with a close friend?"
Note: The sample split is based on answers to "famper3" (see notes to figure 5.4).

with their independently living children—perhaps because of that child's romantic relationships.[32]

I have been unable to find published studies that report trends in Americans' experiences of social demands or tribulations.

A closing note on the topic of tribulations: I have treated them here as the "loss" side of the social ledger. But another view of this topic is that the key distinction we need to draw is not between positive and negative relationships, but between being socially engaged or not. Socially isolated people lack both support and demands from others; socially integrated people have plenty of both. In any event, little seems to have changed in this regard over the years covered here.

Conclusions

Without dwelling (yet again!) on the thinness of the data, they suggest that:

- From 1970 to 2010, few American adults—well under one in ten is a rough estimate—reported a lack of personal material or psychological support.[33]

**Figure 5.6   Respondents Who Reported Serious Trouble with a Child in
the Past Year, by Whether Respondent Had a Child Under
Twenty-Five Years Old at Home—GSS**

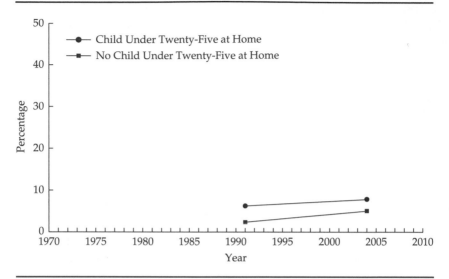

Source: Author's compilation based on data from GSS item "famper4."
Questions: "What about family and personal relationships? During the last year, did
you . . . have serious trouble with a child?"
Notes: The sample split—respondent has or does not have a child under twenty-five at
home—is only approximate. While any household resident under eighteen is clearly a
child, the way items are coded in the GSS makes it difficult to be certain which household
members are children of the respondent. In some cases, the eighteen- to twenty-four-
year-old in question may be the respondent himself or herself or a spouse. I reran the
analyses, dropping respondents under the age of thirty to avoid that confounding, and
the results were essentially the same.

- Americans later in this period were about as likely as Americans
  earlier in the period to report having social support. If there is a
  trend, it was probably toward people reporting or expecting *more*
  emotional help.

- Overall, Americans became no more likely—and in some situations
  less likely—to say that they suffered tribulations from their spouses,
  relatives, or friends.

- Americans' reports of problems and breakups with romantic partners (but not spouses) increased and may have disrupted other relationships.

═ Chapter 6 ═

Feeling Connected

To THIS POINT, the focus has been on how socially connected Americans said they were. We turn now to Americans' *feelings* about their connections to family and friends. To be sure, almost all survey questions are subjective. Even those that ask respondents to number their friends, to report how often they see a parent, or to say how much they can rely on kin get replies that are in significant part reflections of the interviewees' worldviews (such as what they consider a friendship), wishes (for example, how often they feel they should see their parents), and expectations (their ideas perhaps about what kin owe one another). Nonetheless, researchers design such questions to get at actual behavior. This chapter looks at more explicitly subjective issues: what people feel about their relationships (or the absence thereof), and later, what they feel about themselves as social beings.

A caution: some learned observers of American culture argue that after the 1960s, Americans became more introspective and expressive—that a "therapeutic" ethos emerged.[1] If this were true, we might expect Americans to have become more self-absorbed, perhaps more self-critical and confessional, over time. I cannot take such a development into account here.

Loneliness

The most directly relevant feeling is, of course, that lonely feeling. The one consistent finding of the sizable literature on loneliness (especially, but not only, among the elderly) is that whether people say that they feel lonely is only *weakly* associated whether they are actually isolated.[2] There is a key exception to this statement: people who are unmarried and have no romantic partner are notably likelier to say that they are lonely. (To quote Roy Orbison: "Now only the lonely/Know the heartaches I've been through/Only the lonely/Know I cry and cry for you.") Partners aside, people who report small personal networks—and in some studies also people who live alone—are only slightly more likely, if at all, than other people to report feelings of loneliness. The connection between the two is certainly far too weak to assume that the same people both feel lonely and are alone.

This finding also shows up in the GSS. In 1996 the survey asked, "Now I'm going to read a list of different feelings that people sometimes have. After each one, I would like you to tell me on how many days you have felt this way during the past seven days . . . felt lonely?" That year the GSS asked the same respondents the battery of questions about how often they spent social evenings with relatives, neighbors, and friends (see chapter 4). Answers to the "social evening" questions do *not* substantially correlate with answers to the "loneliness" question.[3]

For all the interest in loneliness, there appears to be little national survey data that would permit us to draw trends. Figures 6.1 and 6.2 present a handful of not fully comparable series. In figure 6.1, the question is: "During the past few weeks, did you ever feel . . . very lonely or remote from other people?" The line shows the percentage saying "yes." I include two pre-1970 points, both to add more observations and to highlight the effects of national tragedies. The two highest points come from surveys done in the two weeks after the assassination of President Kennedy and the two weeks after the attacks of September 11, 2001. (Complicating the picture is the fact that the lowest points on the graph are from surveys conducted by Gallup and the highest ones are from surveys conducted by NORC.) Psychometricians have found that answers to "loneliness" questions tend to be highly correlated with answers to questions designed to measure depression, so the two surges of expressed loneliness may reflect surges of depression following national tragedies.

Figure 6.2 presents three series. The three-point line with circles represents answers to the Louis Harris probe, "Now I'd like to read you a list of things that may have affected you in the last month. For each, please tell me if it's affected you in the last month, or not . . . being lonely." It shows no trend. The two-point line with diamonds represents the World Values Survey question asking respondents whether they had "ever felt lonely or remote from other people" in the prior two weeks. In 1982, 16 percent said "yes" and in 1990, 18 percent did—no trend. The upper line displays answers to variations of the question "How much is loneliness a problem [for you personally]," displaying the percentage who said that it was a problem; the line shows a clear upward trend. Unfortunately, the specific questions and the survey organizations represented in that line, unlike the other two, varied somewhat from year to year. We might have expected some increase in loneliness reports simply because unmarried people report more loneliness, and more American adults were unmarried in the 2000s than in the 1970s. The higher line in figure 6.2 suggests a possible rise in concerns about loneliness,[4] but the set of results do not support a trend in expressions of loneliness.

Figure 6.1   Respondents Who Felt Lonely in the Past Few Weeks—NORC and Gallup

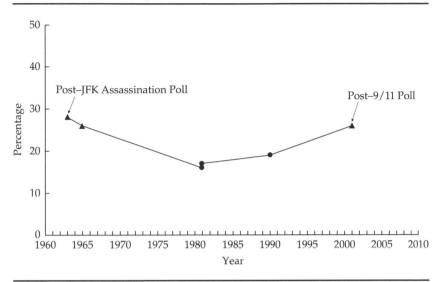

Sources: Author's compilation. 1963: National Opinion Research Center (NORC) via iPoll, USNORC.63KENN.R34D; 1965: NORC via iPoll, USNORC.65SRS.R05D; 1981a: Gallup via iPoll, USGALLUP.030082.R122D; 1981b and 1990: Gallup for the World Values Survey website; 2001: NORC via iPoll, USNORC.01NTS1.Q10.
Question: 1963 and 1965: "(Here are a few questions we have been asking people regularly during the last few years, and we'd like to get your answers now. We are interested in the way people are feeling these days.) During the past few weeks, did you ever feel . . . very lonely or remote from other people?" 1981a, 1981b, and 1990: "(We are interested in the way people are feeling these days.) During the past few weeks, did you ever feel: very lonely or remote from other people?" 2001: "(Here are a few questions we have been asking people regularly during the last few years, and we'd like to get your answers now.) During the past weeks did you ever feel . . . very lonely or remote from other people?"
Notes: (1) The NORC points are marked by triangles, the Gallup points by dots. (2) Respondents to the fall 2001 NORC survey were reinterviewed several weeks later; 24 percent said "yes."

Feelings About Relatives

Americans continued to affirm their commitment to family. The WVS asked, from 1990 through 2006, how important various "aspects" of life— including family, friends, and work—were to respondents: "very important," "rather important," "not very important," or "not at all important." Table 6.1 shows the results. With little variation, over 92 percent of Americans rated family as very important. (I will discuss friends later.) We are with this measure at a "ceiling effect," unable to detect any mean-

Figure 6.2   Respondents Who Said They Were Lonely in the Last Month or That Loneliness Was a Problem—Varied Sources

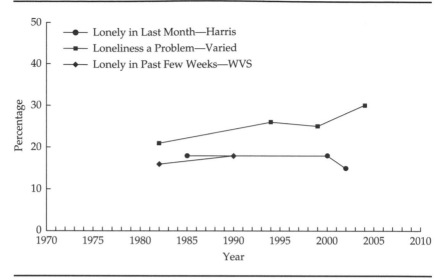

Sources: Author's compilation. (1) Lonely in last month: Harris via iPoll, USHARRIS. 102885.R09, USHARRIS.102500.R1J, USHARRIS.121802.R1M; (2) loneliness a problem: varied, all via iPoll, Chilton Research Services for ABC News/*Washington Post*, USABCWASH1982-763250; 1994: FGI Research, for AARP, USFGI.94AGE.RC06C; 1999: Harris Interactive, for National Council of the Aging, USHARRIS.00AGING.R420C; 2004: FGI Research, for AARP, USAARP.06AGING.RH06C; (3) lonely in past few weeks: WVS online, question A013.

Questions: (1) Harris: "(Now I'd like to read you a list of things that may have affected you in the last month. For each, please tell me if it's affected you in the last month, or not) . . . being lonely." (2) Varied: 1982: "(I'm going to read you some health-related problems that people sometimes have. For each, will you please tell me how much of a problem it is for you personally: a very serious problem, a serious problem, a minor problem, or no problem at all.) . . . loneliness." 1994: "(I'm going to read you some problems that other people have mentioned to us. For each, would you tell me if it is a serious problem, somewhat of a problem, or not a problem for you personally?) How much of a problem is . . . loneliness . . . for you personally?" 1999: "(I'm going to read you some problems that other people have mentioned to us. . . . Would you tell me whether it is a very serious problem, a somewhat serious problem, or not a problem at all for you personally?) . . . loneliness." 2004: "(Now I'm going to read you some problems that other people have mentioned to us. For each, would you tell me if it is a serious problem, somewhat of a problem, or not a problem for you personally?) How much of a problem is . . . loneliness?" (3) WVS: "We are interested in the way people are feeling these days. During the past few weeks, did you ever feel . . . very lonely or remote from other people?"

Notes: (1) The Harris "lonely" question is embedded in a long list of conditions, such as frequent noise, hassles from a boss, and not enough money. (2) WVS: In the online database, the 1990 results were coded 18.5 percent "yes" and 81.5 percent "system missing." I assumed that this was an error and treated the 81.5 percent as "no."

Table 6.1   Respondents Who Rate Aspects of Life As
            Very Important—WVS

	1990	1995	1999	2006
Family	92%	95%	95%	95%
Work	62	56	54	33
Friends	54	70	64	60

Source: Author's compilation.

ingful upward movement. Such consistency may seem trivial and
clichéd, but it contrasts with Americans' ratings of work: In 1990, 62 percent said that work was very important, but by 2006 only 33 percent did.
Americans' emotional attachment to family stayed high and drew increasingly ahead of that major competitor, work.[5]

From 1973 through 1994, the GSS asked respondents how much satis
faction they got from various "areas of life." Figure 6.3 shows the results
for family: with about 43 percent, plus or minus 6 percent, saying that

Figure 6.3   Respondents Who Get a Very Great Deal of Satisfaction from
             Family Life—GSS

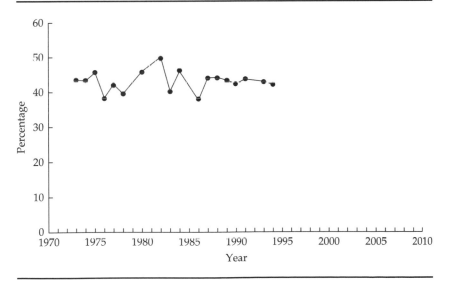

Source: Author's compilation based on data from GSS item "satfam."
Question: "For each area of life I am going to name, tell me the number that shows how
much satisfaction you get from that area . . . your family life." Answers range from 1
(very great deal) to 7 (none).

they got a "great deal" of satisfaction in these areas, there is no change.[6] The DDB Needham organization posed a related question for a few years, asking respondents to agree or disagree with the statement, "Our family is close-knit [more than most families]." Little changed between the mid-1970s and 1984, with about two-thirds "generally" or "definitely" agreeing.[7]

Between 1989 and 2006, the GSS three times asked respondents whether and how they would prefer to change the way they spent their time, including whether they wanted to spend much more, a bit more, the same, less, or much less "time with your family." Telling an interviewer that one wishes for more family time, aside from seeming like the socially appropriate answer, may reflect the respondent's feeling of being short of time. But it should also indicate how much the respondent wants to be with his or her family. The results are striking, as displayed in figure 6.4. The percentage who said that they wished to spend "much more" time rose from 33 to 43 to 55 percent. This increase is in major part due to respondents less often answering "a bit more" and more often answering "much more." (If we look only at the percentage saying either "a bit" or "more" time, the trend line is 75, 81, and 83 percent—a less striking change.) Another caveat is that this question was asked face-to-face by interviewers in 2006 but on self-administered questionnaires in 1989 and 1998; we can suspect that, face-to-face, interviewees might give more familistic answers. Still, the general trend is robustly upward. Taking into account other factors, including how many hours respondents worked, respondents' claims to want more—especially "much more"—time with their family still show an increase.[8]

Another potential indicator of Americans' interest in family is the way they answered a GSS question I first mentioned in chapter 5: "As you know, many older people share a home with their grown children. Do you think this is generally a good idea or a bad idea?" Figure 6.5 shows the percentage of respondents (distinguishing the never-married from those who had ever been married) who said that it was a good idea. The overall percentage approving rose from around 35 percent in the 1970s to about 50 percent in the 2000s, although the increase was slight among the never-married.[9] Both respondents who themselves lived in a three-generation household—about 5 percent did—and those who did not increased their support, and so did the young and the old. The elderly were more dubious about the idea than younger respondents, although their antipathy waned over the decades.

Finally, on feelings about families, Gallup has occasionally asked its respondents, "What is your favorite way of spending an evening?" and let them offer their own answers. The advantage of this item is that it is free-form: answers are not constrained by the pollster's categories. The disadvantage is that the interviewer or coder must afterwards sort the

Figure 6.4   Respondents Who Want to Spend Much More Time with Family—GSS

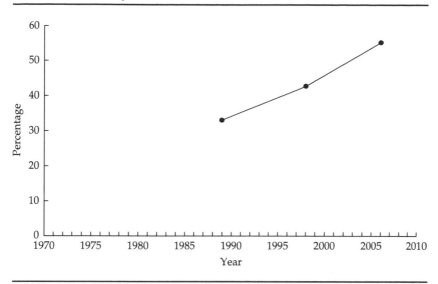

Source: Author's compilation based on data from GSS item "timefam."
Question: "Suppose you could change the way you spend your time, spending more on some things and less on others. Which of these things on the following list would you like to spend more time on, which would you like to spend less time on, and which would you like to spend the same amount of time as now? . . . time with your family." Answers range from 1 (spend much more) to 5 (spend much less).
Note: In 1989 and 1998, the question was asked in a SAQ, in a battery that included questions about time spent on "paid work" and on "household work" before asking about family. In 2006 interviewers asked respondents the same order of questions while presenting each with a card listing the response categories.

answers into categories, and Gallup's categories shifted over the years, at least until recently.[10] Nonetheless, gross trends can be seen in figure 6.6, which displays those "favorite ways" of greatest interest to us: watching television, being home with the family, and one of the answers that entailed seeing friends or relatives. (Other noteworthy response categories are: reading—averaging 13 percent in the 1960s surveys and 10 percent in the two surveys of the 2000s; "resting" or "relaxing"—11 percent and 8 percent, respectively; and going out to dinner, movies, or theater— 8 percent and 10 percent.) Because the results are so erratic, I fit "smoothers" for each of the three series in figure 6.6 to highlight the general trends.[11]

The numbers indicate that over the years fewer respondents said that watching television or videos was their favorite way to spend an evening,

**Figure 6.5   Respondents Who Say It Is a Good Idea for Older People to
Live with Grown Children, by Marital History—GSS**

Source: Author's compilation based on data from GSS item "aged."
Question: "As you know, many older people share a home with their grown children. Do
you think this is generally a good idea or a bad idea?"
Note: About 16 percent of all respondents over all the years volunteered, "it depends,"
with the percentage growing over time. I treated that answer as a "no" for purposes of
this analysis, thereby understating the affirmative trend.

and more respondents said that they preferred being home with their
families.[12] Fewer offered visiting or entertaining friends or relatives,
which would be consistent with the decline in entertaining we saw in previous chapters.

However, these data do not necessarily tell us how Americans *actually*
spent their evenings; for example, actual television watching did not
decline.[13] Similarly, chapter 3 presented mixed evidence about whether
Americans in fact spent more time in the evenings with their families.
Survey respondents reported fewer events with their children, for example, and even less time spent watching television together, although the
time-budget studies suggest that parents spent somewhat more "quality time" with their children. Overall, the surge in favoring evenings
with the family that we see in figure 6.6 does not seem to be matched in
the data about behavior. What should we make of that? Perhaps it indicates guilt—respondents in effect saying, "I can't, but I *should* spend more
time with my family"; or perhaps it reflects an increasingly strong social

**Figure 6.6   Respondents' Favorite Ways to Spend an Evening
(Original Points and "Smoothed" Trends)—Gallup**

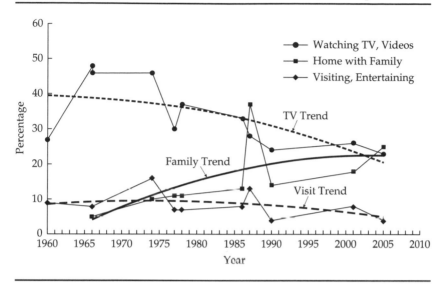

Source: Author's compilation based on data from Gallup Brain, searched by question wording (also available from iPoll).
Question: "What is your favorite way of spending an evening?"
Notes. (1) As discussed in the text, the coding categories shifted over time, perhaps stabilizing in the later years. (2) Gallup also asked this question in 1998 (available from iPoll), but collected multiple responses, about 1.7 per interviewee, making its inclusion unworkable. (It is not clear from the questionnaire in that year whether answers were coded in order of preference.)

norm for family time—"I can't, but I *want* to spend more time with my family"; or perhaps it means that family time became more rewarding— "I can't, but I *enjoy* spending time with my family." Interpretations such as these, at minimum, suggest that Americans' feelings toward their families strengthened, as did the value they put on family time.

Feelings About Friends

Americans value friendships less than family, according to Gallup polls, but about as highly as they value religion, work, and money (and more than they value leisure, hobbies, or community activities).[14] The WVS surveys displayed in table 6.1 suggest that over the course of the 1990s and 2000s Americans' valuing of friends stayed at roughly the same high level.

Although no one seems to have asked Americans if they were satisfied with the number of relatives they had, between 1990 and 2003 Gallup asked Americans if they were satisfied with the number of *friends* they had or whether they wanted more. In the four polls in which the question was asked, about 75 percent, plus or minus three points, answered that they were "satisfied" with the number of friends they had; there is no up or down trend.[15] Other data suggest that the flat trend stretches from 1986 to 2009.[16] We can peer back even earlier, using the *Inner American* surveys, which asked respondents, "Do you feel you have as many friends as you want, or would you like to have more friends?" In both 1957 and 1976, about 40 percent said that they would like to have "more" friends—fewer than the Gallup percentages, although the two sets of surveys are hard to compare.[17]

It is important to realize that respondents who tell interviewers that they would like to have more friends do not, on average, currently lack friends. The GSS in 2000 and 2002 asked, "In the last twelve months . . . have you . . . tried to meet new people for social purposes?" Sixty percent said "no," and about 15 percent said "one or two times." Strikingly, it was the respondents who had already claimed, in answer to other questions, to be socially connected—they had said that they were in regular contact with many people or that they felt "close enough to discuss personal or important problems" with many people—who tended to report having tried to meet new people. Respondents who described themselves as isolated were *not* especially likely to say that they searched for friends.[18] This finding is consistent with psychologists' assumption that people differ a lot in sociability and thus those who have more friends look for yet more friends.

While Americans seemed not to have altered their feelings about the number of friends they had, their feelings about the quality of those friendships may be another matter. Figure 6.7 presents three relevant series. The GSS asked respondents to rate how satisfied they were with the closeness of their friendships; it is the lowest line in the figure. As with family satisfaction, there is no systematic change between 1973 and 1994.[19] The middle line in figure 6.7 tells a different story. Four times the Roper survey asked respondents, "Now here is a list of a number of different things. Would you go down that list and for each one tell me how satisfied with it you are or whether it doesn't apply to you? . . . The friends you've made. Are you completely satisfied with [the friends you've made], fairly well satisfied with [the friends you've made], not too satisfied with [the friends you've made], or not at all satisfied with [the friends you've made]?" The Roper data show a clear decline in the percentage who said that they were "completely" satisfied on this score. (And the percentage who said that they were "not too" satisfied or "not at all" satisfied rose from 4 to 10 percent). It is hard to say why the two series diverge so sharply.[20] The GSS probe is more clearly focused on relationships. The top line in the figure shows the results from Gallup's

Figure 6.7   Respondents Who Say They Are Satisfied with Their Friendships—Gallup, Roper, GSS

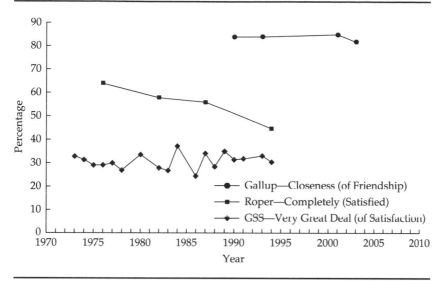

Sources: Author's compilation. (1) Gallup: Gallup polls, except for 1993 (PSRA), all via iPoll, USGALLUP.90FRND.R03, USPSRA.93JUN1.R47, USGALLUP.01DC06.R44, USGALLUP.03DBR11.R22; (2) Roper: Roper and Roper Starch Worldwide Polls, via iPoll, USROPER.76-7.R37F, USROPER.82-7.R61F, USROPER.87-7.R61F, USROPER.94REC.R01C; (3) GSS: GSS item "satfrnd."
Questions: (1) Gallup: "Are you satisfied with the closeness of your relationships with your friends, or would you like to have closer relationships?" (2) Roper: "Now here is a list of a number of different things. (Card shown to respondent.) Would you go down that list and for each one tell me how satisfied with it you are or whether it doesn't apply to you? . . . The friends you've made . . . are you completely satisfied with [the friends you've made], fairly well satisfied with [the friends you've made], not too satisfied with [the friends you've made], or not at all satisfied with [the friends you've made]?" (3) GSS: "For each area of life I am going to name, tell me the number that shows how much satisfaction you get from that area . . . your friendships." Answers range from 1 (very great deal) to 7 (none).
Note: PSRA was established in 1989 by a group from Gallup, so we can assume continuity in procedures.

question that addressed respondents' satisfaction with the *closeness* of their friendships. The rates of reported satisfaction were very high and hardly budged from 1990 to 2003. Two of the three sources, including the one that scholars trust most, show no change.

Finally, we can look at the GSS question about wanting to spend more time with—in this case—"your friends." Two lines appear in figure 6.8 telling slightly different stories. The lower line is the percentage of respondents who said that they would like to spend "much more" time with friends. Unlike their responses about wanting more time with their

Figure 6.8   Respondents Who Say They Want to Spend (Much) More Time with Friends—GSS

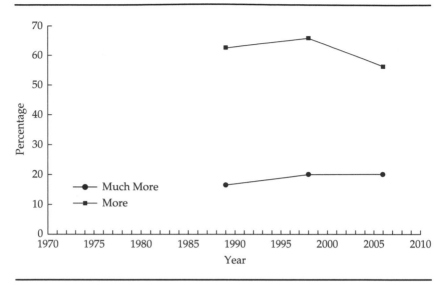

Source: Author's compilation based on data from GSS item "timefrnd."
Question: "Suppose you could change the way you spend your time, spending more on some things and less on others. Which of these things on the following list would you like to spend more time on, which would you like to spend less time on, and which would you like to spend the same amount of time as now? . . . time with your friends." Answers range from 1 (spend much more) to 5 (spend much less).
Note: In 1989 and 1998, the question was asked in a SAQ, in a battery that included questions about time spent on "paid work" and "household work" before asking about family and friends. In 2006 interviewers asked respondents the same order of questions while presenting each with a card listing the response categories.

families (figure 6.4), the percentage saying that they wanted much more time with friends barely changed. The higher line adds together wanting "much more" time with friends and wanting "a bit more" time. That percentage dropped six points between 1998 and 2006, after rising by three points from 1989. The simple gloss is that there was little change in respondents' expressed desire to spend more time with friends.[21] In both 1989 and 2006, just over half of respondents wanted to spend more time with *both* family and friends; the rest, especially in 2006, preferred to get more family time over getting more friend time.[22] The upshot is that Americans clearly expressed more interest in family time—either because they valued it more or because they felt time constraints more—while their interest in friends probably did not change (the evidence is mixed).

Feelings About Oneself

This book's final take on what happened to American relationships is a look at how Americans felt about *themselves*. Did Americans increasingly or decreasingly consider themselves to be sociable or not, to be friendly or shy? Did Americans' social personalities change?

Most personality research describes individuals by the answers that they give to questions. Some techniques involve hiding the purpose of the questions and hoping that respondents unwittingly reveal their personalities. How much that succeeds is unclear. Measuring people according to the personality scheme dominant in psychology these days—the "Big Five" or "Five-Factor Model" of personality dimensions—employs a transparent set of questions that ask people to rate themselves on adjectives such as "extraverted, enthusiastic," and "anxious, easily upset."[23] Several websites provide self-tests.[24]

For all this personality testing, we have very little evidence on how Americans' personalities may have shifted over time. On the subject of sociability—psychologists might prefer to use the terms "extraversion" and "agreeableness" (two of the "Big Five" dimensions)—there appears to be virtually nothing to answer the question of whether Americans changed.[25] In this section, I consider a couple of fragments of evidence.

In both 1990 to 1992 and 2001 to 2003, the National Comorbidity Studies posed three wordy questions assessing how much intimacy respondents felt with other people. (Again, we can only compare eighteen- to fifty-four-year-olds across both surveys.) The first question asked:

> Next, I will read three statements and ask how much each one sounds like you. First, "I find it relatively easy to get close to other people. I am comfortable depending on others and having them depend on me. I don't worry about being abandoned or about someone getting too close to me." How much does this sound like you—a lot, some, a little, or not at all?

In figure 6.9, the line with circles shows the percentage of those who answered that these descriptions of easily getting close to others were either true of them "a lot" or "some[what]." We see negligible change. (The percentage who said "a lot" rose slightly from 28 to 32 percent.)

The other National Comorbidity Studies questions are phrased negatively. The second asks respondents whether this statement described them:

> I am somewhat uncomfortable being close to others. I find it difficult to trust them completely and difficult to depend on them. I am nervous when anyone gets too close to me.

Figure 6.9   Respondents Who Affirm Their Capacity for Intimacy (Eighteen- to Fifty-Four-Year-Olds)—National Comorbidity Survey

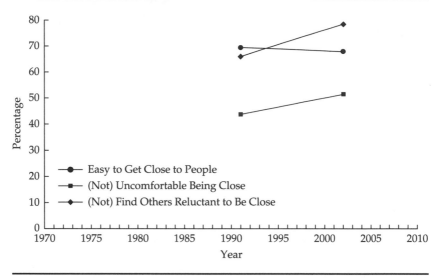

Sources: Author's compilation based on data from the National Comorbidity Survey.
Questions: "Next, I will read three statements and ask how much each one sounds like you." (1) "First, 'I find it relatively easy to get close to other people. I am comfortable depending on others and having them depend on me. I don't worry about being abandoned or about someone getting too close to me.' How much does this sound like you—a lot, some, a little, or not at all?" (2) "I am somewhat uncomfortable being close to others; I find it difficult to trust them completely and difficult to depend on them. I am nervous when anyone gets too close to me." (3) "I find that others are reluctant to get as close as I would like. I often worry that people who I care about do not love me or won't want to stay with me. I want to merge completely with another person, and this desire sometimes scares people away."
Notes: (1) The figure shows the percentages saying "some" or "a lot" to the first question and then saying "not at all" to the other two. (2) The weights are "P2WTV3" for 1990 to 1992 and "NCSRWTLG" for 2001 to 2003, although different weights seem to make little difference. The sample size for these questions for the first wave is (weighted) about 5,380, and for the second wave 4,075. (3) The sample is restricted to eighteen- to fifty-four-year olds to make the two years comparable.

The bottom line shows that the percentage answering that this sounded "not at all" like them rose moderately, from 44 to 51 percent.

Finally, the line with diamonds displays those who answered the third question by saying that the following description sounded "not at all" like them:

> I find that others are reluctant to get as close as I would like. I often worry that people who I care about do not love me or won't want to stay with

me. I want to merge completely with another person, and this desire sometimes scares people away.

The percentage of respondents who *rejected* this description of themselves as unloved rose from 66 percent around 1991 to 78 percent in 2001. The implication of these data is that little changed in Americans' reporting of themselves as persons able to be "close" to others and that any global change was probably in the direction of greater social self-confidence.

Trusting "Most People"

For decades, many scholars have studied another dimension of Americans' subjective social feelings: how "trusting" they are of other people in general, usually as indicated by answers to the question, "Generally speaking, would you say that most people can be trusted or that you can't be too careful in life?" or variants of it. I briefly discussed this question in chapter 2, noting that items such as this, not being about family or friends but essentially about strangers, may not belong in this book. In fact, the GSS has for over thirty years tracked answers to this and two similar questions (asking whether most people are helpful and whether most people are fair; see notes to figure 6.10), and the results show that respondents who answer in a trusting fashion tend to report having more friends and spending more sociable evenings than those who answer distrustfully—but *not by much*.[26] In 1987 most of the respondents who picked the *dis*trustful options in all three questions nonetheless listed three or more people with whom they discussed "important matters," and over the years highly *dis*trusting respondents reported spending social evenings with friends as frequently as did respondents who gave trusting replies to all three questions.[27] Thus, people's answers to the trust questions are at best weakly connected to the descriptions they give of their social lives.

Still, many scholars, including those who originated this line of research over a half-century ago, see it as a measure of respondents' (anti-) social personalities, so it is worth at least a glance. Respondents' likelihood of giving trusting answers seems to have risen from the 1940s into the 1960s and 1970s, and then dropped steadily.[28] Figure 6.10 displays the most comprehensive set of such data, from the GSS. Other, more partial data series with the same questions are roughly consistent.[29]

The line with diamonds in figure 6.10 corresponds to the most frequently studied (and debated) question about whether most people can be trusted; it shows a roughly ten-point drop. The line with circles shows the trend for the question about whether people try to be helpful or selfish; the percentage picking "helpful" slid about four points. The line with squares charts the question about whether people try to be fair; that

Figure 6.10   Respondents Giving More Trusting Answers to Three Trust Questions—GSS

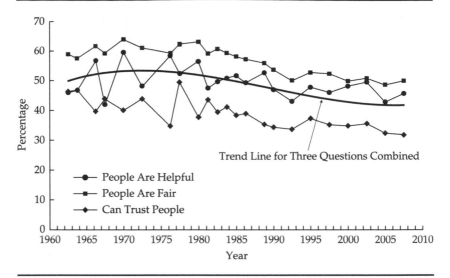

Source: Author's compilation based on data from GSS items labeled "helpful," "fair," and "trust."

Questions: (1) "Would you say that most of the time people try to be helpful, or that they are mostly just looking out for themselves?" (2) "Do you think most people would try to take advantage of you if they got a chance, or would they try to be fair?" (3) "Generally speaking, would you say that most people can be trusted, or that you can't be too careful in life?"

Notes: (1) Respondents who volunteered something like "it depends"—about 5 percent—were so coded. (2) The summary "smoother" is the result of this process: Each respondent received a one for each of the three questions he or she answered in the affirmative—helpful, fair, trustworthy—and a zero for any other answer, yielding a scale from zero to three. I plotted the time trend for the percentage of respondents each year who scored two or three—not shown, for readability—and then fit a quadratic equation to that line. The heavy smoother is that quadratic fit.

declined about ten points. The thick line in the middle of figure 6.10 derives from combining the three questions and then "smoothing" the trend. Trusting answers clearly declined after the early 1980s. Closer analysis of the data reveals that the trend is a result of later-born cohorts giving more suspicious answers than earlier-born cohorts.

To what extent does this trend reflect the average American becoming a more distrustful personality type and to what extent does it reflect Americans' reactions to changes in the world around them—to crime, social unrest, greater ethno-racial diversity, and so on? The research literature provides no clear answer.[30] But the trend probably has more to do with Americans' views of *public* life than with their ties to family and friends. Indeed, we might speculate that immersion in the private worlds of family and friends goes together with alienation from the public world.[31]

Conclusions

The data available on how Americans felt about their social ties and about their social selves suggest the following tentative conclusions. Comparing the later to the earlier years of the 1970 to 2010 period:

- Americans' expressions of loneliness remained the same or perhaps increased slightly; the evidence is mixed.

- Americans became likelier to say that they valued family life—and even that they valued living in a three-generation household.

- Americans felt roughly as satisfied with their families.

- Americans valued friendships to about the same degree.

- Americans remained about as satisfied with the number and quality of their friendships.[32]

- Americans described themselves as socially engaged types of personalities to the same extent, if not more.

- Americans expressed less trust of the general category, "most people."

═ Chapter 7 ═

Conclusions and Speculations

THE QUESTION that this book has posed is whether and how Americans' relationships with family and friends changed between 1970 and 2010. The short answer, based on a canvass of published research and available survey data, is: not much. Some of the ways in which Americans engaged with people in their immediate circles changed, but the intimacy and support of close family and friendship ties stayed about the same. Few Americans were socially isolated, and the percentage of those who were did not increase. The number of family and friends with whom people reported being close stayed about the same. Americans got together with one another in set-aside home activities like dinner parties less often, but they communicated with one another electronically more often. Americans expected to get about as much help from family and friends as they had earlier. And American feelings about their social relationships stayed about the same or became more upbeat. (Chapters 3 through 6 all conclude with a list of more specific and nuanced findings.) One implication of these conclusions is that what Hua Wang and Barry Wellman have labeled the contemporary "panic [about] social connectivity" in America is unfounded.[1]

I would caution, however, that accepting this answer requires faith in survey data. A lot of knotty problems challenge that faith, some of which I reviewed in chapter 2—problems ranging from sampling and question wording to recording errors. Furthermore, questions asked in different years are often only roughly comparable. Researchers like to "improve" survey items over time, which is a worthy goal, but one that makes tracking historical change difficult. The data are sparse, and where comparable measures do exist, they often cover only two or three points in time. Can we really conclude something about change—or an absence of change—in Americans' social relations over the last forty years from, say, comparing a question asked in 1983 to one approximately like it asked in 1997? Furthermore, results in any particular year may differ from those of another year for idiosyncratic reasons—because of historical events, such as a recession or national crisis, or because of methodological variations, such as the question's location in a survey, a shift from in-person to telephone interviews, or simple sampling fluctuations—rather than because of social developments. And even when we have more questions over time, we worry about confounding changes over the same period, such as the decline in response rates.[2] Such concerns require that we treat the conclusions with caution rather than certainty. But the survey data provide us with the best evidence we have—really, the *only* evidence—of what happened.

Assuming the conclusions in chapters 3 through 6 are roughly correct, I turn in this chapter to a consideration of the sorts of large-scale social changes that altered—or may have altered, or perhaps *should* have altered—Americans' ties to family and friends: first, technological developments, most specifically the arrival and expansion of the Internet; second, demographic changes, the drop in the birthrate, and the delay of marriage; third, economic stagnation and increased employment of wives and mothers; and fourth, a residual category of cultural change. I then turn to look again at how people's social relations could be so relatively unchanging in changing circumstances—the argument about adjustment and resilience that I introduced in chapter 1.

Explanations

Chapter 1 covers some of the reasons we might have expected Americans' personal relationships to have changed between 1970 and 2010. The evidence in this book cannot be conclusive about these arguments; I have not undertaken the systematic modeling that causal determinations would require. But the data are suggestive.

Technology: Electronic Communications

Views of electronic media are often polarized. On the one hand, we can read, as we did in chapter 1, William Deresiewicz's cri de coeur: "We have given our hearts to machines, and now we are turning into machines"; or read that "[Professor] Nie asserted that the Internet was creating a broad new wave of social isolation in the United States, raising the specter of an atomized world without human contact or emotion."[3] On the other hand, we can read items like this: "Technology," said Rabbi Menachem Creditor, "allows us to connect more deeply to each other. . . . [The] reason [the virtual world] exists in the first place is to get us to connect in the real world."[4] That the invention, development, and widespread adoption of the Internet, including email, was a major social change is obvious—whether measured by money invested and spent, industries overturned, people engaged, time devoted, cultural expressions, or aspects of life touched. How could it *not* affect personal relationships?

The first reports from studies conducted in the 1990s of how Internet use was affecting Americans' social ties were gloomy. They suggested that the early Internet adopters were shunning their family and friends to heavily immerse themselves in escapist virtual fare and connecting, if to anybody at all, to faceless strangers far away. As the research accumulated—and probably more importantly, as Internet use spread from a minority of enthusiasts to a majority of casual users—the picture changed. Indeed, one researcher whose 1995 study had helped prompt such concerns decided in 2001 that those concerns were overblown. A newspaper story about his reversal carried the headline, "Cyberspace Isn't So Lonely After All."[5]

We have only a few over-time studies that can convincingly tie changes in Internet access and use (including social networking) to changes in social behavior. But we do have many studies that compare Internet users to non-users, and frequent users to infrequent users; most of these studies also control for personal traits, providing partial support for the assertion that they test the effects of Internet use itself. Combined and stirred together, the studies suggest these broad-stroke conclusions:[6]

- Using the Internet and email has little effect on average users' level of face-to-face contact. (Particularly sociable people may employ the Internet to expand in-person contacts, and particularly unsociable people may use it to avoid them.)

- Using the Internet and email increases the total volume of contact that people have with others, notably with friends.

- New personal relationships form over the Internet, but that is the exception. Overwhelmingly, people use the new electronic media to sustain or reactivate existing relationships.

- Users of the new electronic media largely believe that using them has enriched their personal relationships.

Based on these assessments, we would expect that the expansion of electronically mediated communications between 1970 and 2010 would have made it easier for Americans to involve themselves with family and friends. Although access to the Internet may have vastly expanded Americans' circle of *acquaintances*—the Facebook "friends" sort of circle—it would not have been a revolution in their personal relationships, just a nudge.

The evidence in this book does not address, much less test, propositions about the role of the new media in personal life. But the friends and family data seem consistent with the conclusion of researchers that the new electronic media enable relationships. For example, trends reported in chapters 3 and 4 suggest that face-to-face contact with relatives and friends may have slumped a bit—the evidence is uncertain—but that total contact rose. (Additional data from the GSS are consistent.[7])

Demographics

Recapping the discussion in chapter 2, between 1970 and 2010 American young adults extended the period of being independent of their parents while remaining untied down by marriage or parenthood. This is a recipe for transitoriness, formation and loss of friendships, avoidance of new kin connections, and all sorts of emotional turmoil. We saw a few signs of this development in chapter 5 in the increasing reports of partner separations and friend difficulties that seem connected to the delay of marriage. Such turmoil also appears in a 1957, 1976, and 1996 study that found increasingly frequent reports of stress around romantic relationships.[8]

Economics and Work

The economic stagnation that most Americans have slogged through since 1970 curtailed careers and hopes and forced American families to work harder. In particular, it helped spur wives into the labor force and to working longer hours. That change has no doubt had complex effects on social relations that are not yet fully understood. For example, employed mothers, it appears, have sustained and even increased involvement with their children, in part by giving less time to household chores, to spouses, and to having friends over.[9] It is reasonable to assume that more hours at work contributed to the decline we saw (chapters 3 and 4) in at-home socializing and in the frequency of set activities with family members.[10] On the other hand, more employment may well have expanded many women's circle of friends and associates. I have not tried to disentangle statistically the possible contributions of various factors, but the patterns we saw—notably the decline in at-home social life but constant or growing out-of-the-home social life—would be consistent with the hypothesis that changing women's roles were key.[11]

Culture

Too often, a cultural explanation is the "invisible hand" pushing a social change that we cannot otherwise explain. A favorite one in this area is growing "individualism"—the suggestion that Americans increasingly live alone or shun people because we have become more individualistic. Whether or not Americans have become more individualistic is a large topic I cannot address here,[12] but since we do *not*, in fact, observe more social isolation or more shunning of family and friends—if anything, we see greater valuation of family and friends (chapter 5)—it is an explanation in search of a fact to explain.

Cultural explanations can be more, however, than invisible hands. There are habits and modes of thought that emerge, develop, spread, and become taken-for-granted "scripts and schemas" for getting along. They may emerge from structural changes and then become autonomous influences. A couple of examples seem appropriate here. First, perhaps women's move to work made it more difficult to entertain people in the (increasingly messy) home and easier instead to meet friends and family outside the home, especially as entrepreneurs catered to the eat-out and take-out market. Once more couples—especially couples who serve as role models—make this practice habitual, then the earlier pattern, perhaps more common in the 1950s, of having friends over for dinner comes to seem less important, or even less fashionable, to all sorts of people. Second, perhaps the young men and especially the young women who increasingly postponed marriage in order to develop professional careers drifted into cohabitation as a solution to romantic longings during their "emerging adulthoods." Cohabitation, which had previously been common among the poor, then became destigmatized and even fashionable, so that more and more middle-class youth started doing it as well. In such examples, structural developments lead to new cultural practices that then spread beyond their origins as new fashions and customs.

But cultural influences also seem capable of emerging on their own, with great consequences. In the long course of history, the rise of bourgeois sentimentality is one example.[13] Another is the diffusion from elites to the general public of notions of "pure" friendships,[14] and a third may be the spread of parenting models that stress the intense "cultivation" of children.[15] Indeed, some cultural patterns may be strong enough that they lead people to resist or reshape technological, economic, and demographic influences on behavior. Such patterns can be said to be robust or resilient.

Resilience

The most striking thing about the data this book has presented and reviewed is how consistent Americans' ties to family and friends were between the 1970s and 2000s. We rarely find differences of more than a handful of percentage points either way that might describe lasting alterations in behavior with lasting personal consequences—yes, Americans entertained less at home and did more phone calling and emailing, but they did not change much on the fundamentals. Substantial change *is* possible; recall the reference in chapter 1 to the changes in social relations following both Russian and Chinese economic restructuring. How can this general stability in personal ties over the last forty years be understood?

Perhaps that stability is only an illusion. Perhaps survey researchers have not addressed the key dimensions of personal relationships. Or they may have addressed the right concerns, but with questions and techniques that yield such inaccurate results that it *appears* as if stability reigned. Nevertheless, when we accumulate the variety of data we have and see where they converge, the conclusion of stability presses on us.

If such stability is an accurate conclusion, how could it be, given the technological, demographic, economic, and cultural developments of the last forty years? One answer is that most of these developments were not, sociologically speaking, so cataclysmic. Compared to, say, the shift from a predominantly farm existence to a predominantly urban way of life, as happened in the United States around the turn of the previous century, or compared to the demographic and political devastation of a total war, as in Europe in the 1940s, the last forty years have been undramatic. Yet the drop in birthrates, the extension of the life span, and especially the delay of marriage and the move of wives into the workforce may be changes on a sufficiently large scale to warrant the expectation of serious consequences.

As I argued in chapter 1 (and in a much earlier book[16]), people try to adapt to changing circumstances so as to protect their most highly valued ends, which include sustaining the volume and quality of their personal relationships—time with children, contact with relatives, a few sources of intimate support. (This means, by the way, that those who are disposed to modest levels of interaction, who are introverts, or who have strained family relations may adapt in ways that keep their social involvements limited.) It appears, for example, that some Americans in the early twentieth century found that the availability of cheap telephone service allowed them to move away from elderly parents—from the farm, say, to town—while still being able to check up on them to about the same extent.[17] The new electronic media of this century may, similarly, allow friendships to thrive even as invitations to dinner dwindle. As another example, research suggests that widows suffer loneliness from losing their husband, but that their involvement with family, friends, and groups rebounds relatively soon in ways that, at least in part, restore the level of social activity they had before their husband died, or got ill, or even became their husband.[18] And I noted earlier (chapter 3) that women who went to work seem to have sustained or even expanded their time with their children by giving up "lesser" things like housecleaning, time with their spouses, and face time with friends.

This last example reminds us that adaptations and adjustments are not costless. If, for example, the use of modern media has allowed Americans to sustain contact with friends and families at the levels they prefer, it has also cost them financially (perhaps $100 to $200 a month for a typical family[19]), and, some argue, it has cost them psychologically in terms of interruptions and distractions. What we may discover, upon deeper analysis, is that the social changes from 1970 to 2010 *did* profoundly implicate social ties—not by changing them very much, but by leading people to do other things to sustain those ties. So perhaps we would see the implications of the societal changes that Americans experienced after 1970, not in the relationships themselves, but in the side effects—in people's time schedules, residential moves, job transfers, leisure-time activities, spending patterns, and so on—of sustaining social ties.

Conclusion

Where Americans' ties go from here cannot be predicted. Sociology is not a forecasting science. The material conditions of life—and cultural fashions—can move in various directions; large shocks may be around the corner. Over the long run—say, the last couple of centuries—Americans' ties to kin have diminished, in number at least, if for no other reason than that families have shrunk in size. In addition, nonkin relationships have probably displaced weaker kinship and local ties—people may now turn to friends instead of cousins, to coworkers instead of neighbors. The friendships that emerge from work, clubs, hobbies, and casual meetings, and that are then sustained by modern affluence and communications, have probably grown in number and kind. In the window of the last forty years, not much has changed, and that continuity probably testifies to the ardor of Americans' ties to their families and friends.

Appendix: Data Sources

ANES: Data from American National Election Studies (http://www. electionstudies.org/), located at Stanford University and the University of Michigan, are available for online analysis at http://sda.berkeley.edu/ and elsewhere.

DDB: The 1977 to 1998 DDB Needham Lifestyle Surveys used by Putnam (2000) were downloaded for analysis from his website (www.bowlinga lone.com). Reports of 1999 to 2003 results are available from *Polling the Nations.* Later data are not available.

Gallup: Results from Gallup polls compiled at the Gallup Brain database are searchable (for a fee) on a database at: http://institution.gallup.com/. They are also available from *iPoll.*

GSS: Data from the General Social Survey, conducted by the National Opinion Research Center (http://www.gss.norc.org/), are available for online analysis at http://sda.berkeley.edu/ and elsewhere.

Harris: Results of surveys by Louis Harris & Associates polling organizations are available via *iPoll.*

iPoll: An archive of public opinion data, the iPoll database is located at the *Roper Center.* The specific tables are noted by tags (for example, USGALLUP.97FB24.R35).

National Comorbidity Studies: (1) National Comorbidity Survey: Baseline (NCS-1), 1990 to 1992, obtained from the Inter-University Consortium for Political and Social Research (ICPSR) at the University of Michigan, study 6693. (2) National Comorbidity Survey Replication (NCS-R), 2001 to 2003, ICPSR study 189.

Polling the Nations: A compilation of thousands of surveys available at: http://poll.orspub.com/.

PSRA: Princeton Survey Research Associates makes selected data available through *iPoll.*

Roper: The results of the surveys conducted by the Roper poll for its regular *Reports* or for customers come either from analyzing the data set of selected items compiled by Brady et al. (2000) or from reports of results in the *iPoll.* In either case, the data are available only through 1994.

Roper Center: The Roper Center for Public Opinion Research at the University of Connecticut is the location of the *iPoll* database (http://www.ropercenter.uconn.edu/).

Saguaro: The Social Capital Benchmark Community Surveys are conducted by the Saguaro Seminar (www.ksg.harvard.edu/saguaro). The data are now stored at the Roper Center.

WVS: The World Value Surveys are a set of parallel surveys now conducted in almost one hundred societies. Five waves were completed between 1981 and 2007. The data are available for online analysis at: http://www.worldvaluessurvey.org/.

═ Notes ═

Preface

1. Most of the facts cited in this paragraph are taken from Wikipedia. On ABC, see Jack Gould, "TV Review: Pro Football Kicks Off in ABC Prime Time," *New York Times*, September 22, 1970; on phone costs, see Noll (1994), fig. 1.

2. Calculated from the online archive page of the *New York Times*. Similarly, the unfortunate metaphor "social capital," used to refer to individuals' social relationships (among many other things), increased exponentially after 1970. Previous uses of the term in the *Times*, as far back as the nineteenth century, appear, upon cursory examination, to refer to much different topics, such as the "capital" (leading city) of sociability or the "social" resources of a society. On the unfortunateness of the term, see Fischer (2005) and Kadushin (2004).

Chapter 1

1. Janet Kornblum, "Study: 25% of Americans Have No One to Confide In," *USA Today*, June 23, 2006; Bharathi Radhakrishnan, "Americans Have Fewer Friends, Researchers Say," ABC News Online, June 23, 2006; Debbie Elliott "Social Isolation: Americans Have Fewer Close Confidantes," NPR, June 24, 2006; Scott Allen, "It's Lonely Out There," *Boston Globe*, June 23, 2006; Ellen Goodman, "Friendless in America," *Boston Globe*, June 30, 2006; Reuters, "Nearly a Quarter of American Adults Have No Close Friends, Survey Finds," *National Post* (Canada), June 27, 2006; Henry Fountain, "The Lonely American Just Got a Bit Lonelier," *New York Times*, July 2, 2006.

2. McPherson, Smith-Lovin, and Brashears (2006).

3. Fischer (2009); McPherson, Smith-Lovin, and Brashears (2009). As is typical in news reports of scientific research, a bland correction did not catch up with an exciting error—and not only in the news media. For example, Thomas Sander and Robert Putnam (2010) note the dispute about the GSS results in a footnote, but proceed as if the original results were fact. The governing board of the GSS was sufficiently puzzled by the findings that it commissioned a 2010 "survey experiment" to figure out what happened in the 2004 survey.

4. Examination of JSTOR, the academic online depository, revealed 207 titles or abstracts referring to "social network(s)" in all the years before 1981, then 335 in the 1980s, 548 in the 1990s, and 362 in the first few years of the 2000s. Proportionally, as well, the increase was quite dramatic. Stephen Borgatti and Pacey Foster (2003), using another type of count, report an exponential increase in sociology articles on social networks from 1970 to 2000.

5. Fischer (1983).

6. Pedahzur and Perliger (2006); Patrick Radden Keefe, "Idea Lab: Can Network Theory Thwart Terrorists?" *New York Times Magazine*, March 12, 2006; Bearman, Moody, and Stovel (2004).

7. Jane E. Brody, "Personal Health," *New York Times*, April 6, 1983.

8. On Packard, see Fischer (1973), although at the time I had not dug out the data on declining mobility; on loneliness, see Fischer and Phillips (1982); on Putnam, see Fischer (2005); on McPherson, Smith-Lovin, and Brashears (2006), see Fischer (2009).

9. See, for example, Giddens (1991) and Gergen (2000).

10. See, for example, Wellman (1979), Fischer (1984), and Friedman (1990).

11. See, for example, Schwartz (2004) and Rosenthal (2005).

12. The association is contingent and complex, but overall strong (Holt-Lunstad, Smith, and Layton 2010). See details in studies such as Thoits (1995); Cornwell and Waite (2009a); Ertel, Glymour, and Berkman (2009); Cohen and Janicki-Deverts (2009); and Umberson, Crosnoe, and Reczek (2010).

13. See, for example, Rook (1984); Leffler, Krannich, and Gillespie (1986); and Antonucci, Akiyama, and Lansford (1998).

14. For poll data, see Fischer (2010, 304, note 105); see also Rosenzweig and Thelen (1998). This is not unlike Americans' tendency to say that things are generally in bad shape, but not the things immediately around them—for example, American schools versus their own children's schools; see, for example, Frank Newport, "Americans Not Convinced That Schools Are in Crisis," Gallup News Service, August 24, 2006, available at: http://www.gallup.com/poll/24244/Americans-Convinced-Local-Schools-Crisis.aspx (accessed November 12, 2010). On this tendency, see Smith (1998).

15. See, for example, Fischer (1984, 2010).

16. Deresiewicz (2009).

17. Stephanie Clifford, "Online, 'a Reason to Keep on Going,' " *New York Times*, June 2, 2009.

18. Katie Hafner, "Texting May Be Taking a Toll," *New York Times*, May 26, 2009.

19. Furstenberg et al. (2004); Settersten, Furstenberg, and Rumbaut (2005).

20. U.S. Bureau of the Census, "Table MS-2: Estimated Median Age at First Marriage, by Sex: 1890 to the Present" (November 2010), available at: http://www.census.gov/population/socdemo/hh-fam/ms2.xls (accessed November 12, 2010).

21. Fischer and Hout (2006, ch. 4); Smock (2000); Reinhold (2010).

22. U.S. Bureau of the Census, "Supplemental Table 1: Percent Childless and Births per 1,000 Women in the Last Year: Selected Years, 1976 to 2006" (August 2008), available at: http://www.census.gov/population/socdemo/fertility/cps2006/SupFertTab1.xls (accessed November 12, 2010).

23. The birthrate plunged from the 1950s to 1972. From 1973 on, however, it fluctuated around 14 or 15 births per 1,000 population, with a net drop of about one between the late 1970s and the 2000s (U.S. Bureau of the Census, *Statistical Abstract 2010*, "Table 78: Live Births, Deaths, Marriages, and Divorces," available at: http://www.census.gov/compendia/statab/2010/tables/10s0078.xls [accessed September 19, 2010]).

24. The phrase is Jeffrey Arnett's (1998, 2004) and has been adopted by other scholars. See, for example, the MacArthur Network on Transitions to Adulthood (http://www.transad.pop.upenn.edu/).

25. Christian Smith's (2009, ch. 2) description of the lives and views of his eighteen- to twenty-three-year-old interviewees captures the turmoil, self-centeredness, and experimental nature of their lives—and their great attention to managing personal relationships.

26. This conclusion is based on running the following analysis in the pooled 2006 and 2008 GSS surveys: among thirty- to sixty-year-olds only (in order to hold age roughly constant), the variables "socrel," "socommun," "socfrend," "B5A1," and "B5A2" X "spaneng" X "Hispanic" yielded tables showing that the Spanish-language interviewees were much likelier to report low levels of social activities and to report themselves as socially reserved than were the English-language interviewees of either Hispanic or non-Hispanic background.

27. Between 1970 and 1966, the additional years of life that an American male of sixty-five could expect increased from 13.0 to 17.0; for a sixty-five-year-old American female, the increase was from 16.8 to 19.7 (U.S. Bureau of the Census, *Statistical Abstract 2010*, "Table 103: Average Number of Years of Life Remaining by Sex, Race, Age," available at: http://www.census.gov/compendia/statab/2010/tables/10s0103.xls (accessed November 12, 2010); National Center for Health Statistics 1975, table 3).

28. Based on Fischer (1982a).

29. Calculated from U.S. Bureau of the Census, *Statistical Abstract 2010*, "Table 583: Labor Force Participation Rates by Marital Status, Sex, and Age," available at: http://www.census.gov/compendia/statab/2010/tables/10s0583.xls (accessed November 12, 2010); see also Cohany and Sok (2007).

30. Putnam (2000, ch. 11) considers whether this change might explain the declines in civic life he describes, but then sets it aside as an explanatory factor, in large part because he sees parallel declines among working and non-working women. This comparison is important but not determinative. The departure of women, especially the more skilled ones, from the neighborhood during the day and from organizational and social activities in the evening would hobble other women's activities as well. See also Costa and

Kahn (2003a) for an analysis that places great explanatory weight on rising work hours for women.

31. Presser (2003, 2004). Harriet Presser (2003, ch. 1) explains why, for technical reasons, there are no good time trends on the volume of irregular work hours, but also why it is very likely that they increased substantially.

32. This is not the place to go over the vast and controversial literature on the economic fortunes of Americans since 1970. It is fair to say that, among middle-class Americans, having two wage-earners seemed necessary to sustain that lifestyle. Also, economic developments, while providing vastly cheaper products of some kinds (food, clothes, and electronics, notably), cost Americans much more in housing, medical care, and college tuition. Survey data show that most Americans' comfort with their financial situation probably deteriorated from 1970 on, even before the economic crisis that unfolded between 2007 and 2008. See Fischer and Hout (2006, ch. 6) for an overview of these points.

33. Swaan (1995).

34. See, for example, Stearns (1999), Stearns and Lewis (1998), and Fischer (2010).

35. *American Heritage Dictionary of the English Language*, 4th edition. I have been wrestling with these ideas for quite a while; see, for example, Fischer et al. (1977, 197ff.) and Fischer (1992, ch. 1).

36. Shklovski, Kraut, and Rainie (2006, 262).

37. Granovetter (1973); Blau and Fingerman (2009).

38. danah boyd, "Will the Real Social Network Please Stand Up?" (July 30, 2009), available at: http://www.futurelab.net/blogs/marketing-strategy-innovation/2009/07/would_real_social_network_plea.html (accessed September 16, 2009).

39. Danching Ruan and his colleagues (1997) replicated (approximately) a survey in Tianjin in 1986 and 1993, using the GSS "important matters" question. They find a drop of about one-third in the size of reported networks and a shift from kin and coworkers to "friends" and "others." They explain the changes as a result of a shift from a spartan, work group–based economy to a flourishing market economy. David O'Brien, Stephen Wegren, and Valeri Patsiorkovsky (2005) and O'Brien and Patsiorkovsky (2006) find that Russian villagers' households and personal networks grew, while their local community involvement dropped, between 1995 and 2003.

40. This observation is based on a search of online databases covering 1990 through mid-2009 that revealed thousands of citations to "social networks" but virtually none about change over time, especially for the United States.

41. Putnam (2000). Note also the important paper by Dora Costa and Matthew Kahn (2003a), which reanalyzes in more advanced models much of the same data Putnam used.

Chapter 2

1. Bearman and Parigi (2004). On this and other methods issues, see Marsden (2010).

2. In a forthcoming book, Barry Wellman reports on research in Toronto that also shows that people who have "very close" social ties may not "discuss important matters" with them—at least, not in the way that question is understood (personal communication, July 18, 2010).

3. This definition is drawn and adapted from Fischer (1982a, 286–88).

4. This definition describes what network analysts call an "egocentric" network; it is defined by who is connected to the central person. The other strategy is to define a "whole" network, as stipulated by the 2009 Wikipedia entry: "A social network is a social structure made of individuals (or organizations) called 'nodes,' which are tied (connected) by one or more specific types of interdependency, such as friendship, kinship, financial exchange, dislike, sexual relationships, or relationships of beliefs, knowledge or prestige" ("Social Network," Wikipedia, available at: http://en.wikipedia.org/wiki/Social_network [accessed September 15, 2009]). Here, one starts with a set of "nodes" in some category (for example, the one hundred largest corporations, or all the students in a classroom) and analyzes the structure of the interconnections among them (say, the number of officers on the boards of directors that the companies share, or the time each child spends playing with another). By contrast, the personal networks I am describing are defined from the focal person outward.

5. See, for example, Killworth et al. (1990).

6. Both phrases are titles of noteworthy books on networks: Jeremy Boissevain's *Friends of Friends* (1974) and Duncan Watts's *Six Degrees* (2003).

7. I refer here to the work of Nicholas Christakis and James Fowler (see, for example, Christakis and Fowler 2009) arguing for substantial network influences—up to the third-order tie—on a variety of outcome variables. For a critique, see Cohen-Cole and Fletcher (2008), among others.

8. See, for example, Rook (1984, 1989), Leffler, Krannich, and Gillespie (1986), Thoits (1995), and Falci and McNeely (2009).

9. Leib (2007).

10. Close associates usually know what one already knows and have what one already has. An important literature on the "strength of weak ties" developed after Mark Granovetter circulated a paper with that name in the early 1970s (Granovetter 1973). The study that generated this insight is *Getting a Job* (Granovetter 1974/1995). Recently, a popular book by Melinda Blau and Karen Fingerman, *Consequential Strangers* (2009), has elaborated and illustrated ideas about weak ties. Considerable research (for example, Lin 1999; Erickson 2003) has developed around a method designed especially to measure respondents' weak ties, the position generator.

11. Some attributes of ties and networks—for example, multiplexity, centrality, inwardness, homophily, density, and between-ness—seem abstruse. They can reveal much about networks, but often require difficult and complex measurement.

12. Sources include the theoretical writings of Georg Simmel, the "sociometric" research pioneered by Jacob Moreno, the role theory promoted by scholars such as Robert Merton, the anthropological work of the Manchester School, and the social-psychological studies of small-group communications. See Freeman (2004) for a wide-ranging intellectual history and Marin and Wellman (2010) for one more focused on recent developments.

13. Lundberg and Steele (1938).

14. Later, in the 1950s, Columbia University sociologists carried out major studies of "personal influence" (see especially Katz and Lazarsfeld 1955; Coleman, Katz, and Menzel 1966). James Coleman (1958–1959) presents the early thinking of the Columbia school about what he calls "relational analysis." But modern practices for surveying individuals' personal networks probably originated in two studies by Edward Laumann conducted in the 1960s—one in the vicinity of Harvard and the other in the Detroit area—in which men were asked to name their best friends (Laumann 1966, 1973). Barry Wellman and I, separately, elaborated on his approach in the 1970s (Wellman 1979; Fischer 1982a).

15. I suppose that creative scholars could try to compare, say, telephone records between the 1970s and the 2000s. In principle, such records could tell us which households were in contact with which other households; they would tell us little about the nature of the calls, of course. Such data have been used, by economic geographers among others, to answer macro-structural questions—for example, to what extent did Los Angeles reduce New York's economic centrality? A "softer" approach draws—as historians of the nineteenth century have done—on collections of correspondence to assess the quality of the writers' bonds. However valuable for some purposes, such an approach wouldn't answer the question of this book.

16. GSS question 368B.

17. Wisconsin Longitudinal Survey question "mv054rer."

18. Krause and Borawski-Clark (1994).

19. National Comorbidity Survey Replication, 2001–2003, question "SN7."

20. McCarty et al. (1997). For the estimate of 291 people, see McCarty et al. (2001); see also Marsden (2005).

21. Here are two examples from the General Social Survey: (1) The most specific GSS network question, used in 1985, 1987, and 2004, is the same one discussed earlier: Has the respondent discussed "important matters" with anyone in the previous six months? The GSS also has regularly asked respondents the vaguer question: "How often [do] you . . . spend a social evening with friends who live outside the neighborhood?" Response categories

range from "almost daily" to "never." In 1985, 83 percent of those who said that they spent such a social evening at least once a month went on later in the interview to name two or more people with whom they discussed important matters. In contrast, only 59 percent of the interviewees who reported spending no more than one social evening a year with friends later named two or more people with whom they discussed important matters.

Table N1 is a fuller table (cases weighted by "compwt"), calculated on Berkeley's SDA data analysis program (http://sda.berkeley.edu/). I percentage the table by the "socfrend" question because that came first in the survey (chi-square = 74; $p < .001$; $V = .16$).

Table N1.   Number of Names Offered on "Important Matters" Question by Frequency of Spending Evening With Friends

On "Important Matters" Question	Spends Social Evenings with Friends Outside the Neighborhood		
	Several Times a Week or More	Once to Several Times a Month	Once a Year or Never
Names no one or only one person	17%	20%	41%
Names two to four persons	57	51	48
Names five or six persons	26	28	11
N	343	923	272

Source: Author's compilation based on General Social Survey.

We would not have expected a full correspondence between the two questions; for example, respondents who discuss "important matters" with kin or neighbors may have little social life outside their neighborhoods, but there is a noteworthy correlation.

(2) In 2002 the GSS asked respondents: (a) "Not counting people at work or family at home, about how many other friends or relatives do you keep in contact with at least once a year?" and (b) "How often do you have any other contact with this ["best friend" previously discussed] besides visiting, either by telephone, letter, fax, or email?" On the surface, there is no logical connection between these two questions, except that the totally contactless and the totally friendless tend to be the same people. Yet there was a modest connection: 17 percent who said they were "in contact" with only one to six people also said they rarely had contact—other than visiting—with their best friends, while just 6 percent of those who claimed thirty-one or more contacts reported communicating with their best friends that rarely. (The GSS items are "numcntct" and "bstcall.") Again, there is no logical necessity for these two to go together, but their association suggests that they both tap general levels of social connectedness.

22. The table here (table N2) shows the association between the GSS item "socfrend" (how often the respondent sees friends outside the neighborhood) and the item "lonely" (how many days the respondent felt lonely in the past week). The questions were asked in 1996, and the cases were weighted by "compwt." The association is not even linear (chi-square = 7, n.s.). See also Dykstra et al. (2005).

Table N2.   Number of Days Respondents Reported Feeling Lonely by Frequency of Spending Evening With Friends

How Many Days a Week Respondent Felt Lonely	Spends Social Evenings with Friends Outside the Neighborhood		
	Several Times a Week or More	Several Times a Year to Several Times a Month	Once a Year or Never
None	51%	58%	55%
One or two days	25	22	18
Three or more days	25	20	27
N	244	590	152

Source: Author's compilation based on General Social Survey.

23. An important but differently purposed approach to network description deserves mention: the "positional" method (see, for example, Lin 1999; Erickson 2003). Interviewers ask respondents if they personally know (and perhaps how well they know) people in different sorts of jobs—lawyer, janitor, and so forth. The resulting measures indicate the occupational span of respondents' networks and tell us about their capacities to mobilize practical help. This technique does not, however, assess the number, character, and intimacy of respondents' personal ties.

24. Katz and Lazarsfeld (1955). Elihu Katz (1957) reviews other studies out of the Columbia school, notably the one by Coleman and his colleagues (1966) *Medical Innovation,* which used variants of this method. Katz and Lazarsfeld (1955, 151) note that "no particularly strong resistance to the furnishing of names and addresses was encountered," which would be far from the case today.

25. Other important studies in this vein include the 1965 study by Edward Laumann (1973), who asked white men in the Detroit area about "the three men who are your closest friends and whom you see most often"; Barry Wellman's 1968 survey of Toronto residents in which he asked them about the persons outside their households to whom they felt "closest" (Wellman 1979); Mark Granovetter's 1969 survey of professional men in Newton, Massachusetts, asking them who had helped them get their job (Granovetter 1973, 1974/1995); and my own 1977–1978 survey of northern Californians (Fischer 1982a) who responded to eleven different requests to list the people with whom they were involved in about eleven possible ways (could

borrow something from, goes out socially with, talks over personal issues, can consult about work, and so on).

26.   Marsden (1987); see also Burt (1984).

27.   I make a long argument for the exchange-based method of studying networks in Fischer (1982a, 285–94). In a line of research somewhat disconnected from the one I have been covering here, Toni Antonucci and her colleagues have studied people's "social convoys," using questions asking about closeness. "Convoy" refers to "family and friends who surround the individual and help in the successful negotiation of life's challenges"—in other words, those people "to whom he or she is related through the exchange of social support." Procedurally, interviewers present respondents with

> a set of three concentric circles with a smaller circle in the center in which the word "you" was written. The respondent was told that the three circles should be thought of as including "people who are important in your life right now" but who are not equally close. Respondents were then asked to think about "people to whom you feel so close that it is hard to imagine life without them." Such persons were entered in the innermost circle of the network diagram. The same procedure was followed for the next circle, described as including "people to whom you may not feel quite that close but who are still very important to you," and for the outer circle, described as including "people whom you haven't already mentioned but who are close enough and important enough in your life that they should be placed in your personal network." (Antonucci and Akiyama 1987, 519–20)

Respondents were then asked questions about the first ten people they named, including descriptions of the individuals and the sort of support they gave and took from the respondent. See also Antonucci, Akiyama, and Lansford (1998) and Antonucci, Akiyama, and Takahashi (2004).

28.   See Bernard et al. (1990); van Sondoren et al. (1990); van Groenou, van Sondoren, and Ormel (1990); and van der Poel (1993a, 1993b); see also Marsden (1990, 2005).

29.   Most researchers cannot devote eleven questions, asked in person, to this task, as we did in the northern California study (Fischer 1982a). Network analysts have therefore searched hard for an efficient set of one, two, or three questions (see, for example, Burt 1984; Marin and Hampton 2007). There is mixed evidence on the interchangeability of various name-eliciting questions. The truly important members of respondents' networks tend to be named in almost any case—although sometimes people forget to list key people, notably their spouses, if not reminded (Fischer 1982a, 289; Stueve and Lein 1979). Relying on a single question, such as the GSS "important matters" item, although less taxing, can often yield a distorted picture of a respondent's personal network. For example, many of the people with whom we enjoy partying are not the same ones with whom we have heart-to-heart talks (see, for example, McCallister and Fischer 1978; Marin 2004; Marin and Hampton 2007; Klofstad, McClurg, and Rolfe 2009; Straits 2000; Bailey and Marsden 1999; and Bearman and Parigi 2004).

30.   Interviewees polled at one time forget (or perhaps refuse) to list some people whom they listed another time. Other factors besides question choice and

respondent recall affect the census of networks that surveys can elicit—interviewer effort and skill, for example. Some are a lot better and some a lot worse than others (see Fischer 1982a, 302; Marsden 2003, 2005; van Tilburg 1998). For all the problems, the saving grace, studies have shown, is that respondents tend to be pretty reliable in listing the most critical people in their core networks. Also, while they do not consistently name the same peripheral members of their networks, these acquaintances and distant kin tend to be socially similar to one another—for example, about the same proportion are male, or drawn from work each time. Thus, the particular list of names that respondents give one time may be notably different the next time, but the descriptions of their networks look about the same. "The stability of the aggregate properties in personal networks is much greater than the stability of the membership in these networks," conclude David Morgan, Margaret Neal, and Paula Carder (1997; see also Brewer 2000; Bell, Belli-McQueen, and Haider 2007)—which is roughly what Lynne McCallister and I concluded in 1978 (McCallister and Fischer 1978).

Once people in respondents' personal networks have been listed, the issue becomes one of how accurately the interviewees can describe who those people are. In a relatively few and limited studies (for example, Katz and Lazarsfeld 1955), researchers find out those answers from the named people themselves. Studies that interview full rosters of groups, such as all the students in a classroom, can get descriptive information from all the nominees. An important example is the "Add Health" national longitudinal survey of high school students that interviews throughout schools (Carolina Population Center 2009). The focal respondents can be relatively accurate about basic facts concerning their alters, such as their ages, although fuzzier about other topics, such as their friends' political leanings. See the summary in Marsden (2005); see also Marsden (1990) and Laumann (1973, ch. 2). On measuring attributes of relationships, see Marsden and Campbell (1984).

31. Survey by *Parents* magazine (May 1987), as reported in Roper Center, iPoll, record USKANE.PM0587.R25B.

32. Fischer (1982b).

33. For example, the next chapter presents the historical trend in answers to the question, "About how often do you socialize with close friends, relatives, or neighbors?" In 1995, Princeton Survey Associates used that question and, on another sample, a variant: "About how often do you visit or spend time with close friends, relatives, or neighbors?" Using "visit or spend time" rather than "socialize" raised the percentage of respondents who gave answers of twice a week or more from 53 to 75 percent (data from Roper Center, iPoll, records USPSRA.95PREV.R19F1 and USPSRA.95PREV.R19F2).

34. For example, in 1986 and in 2002 the GSS asked respondents how often they visited with their closest friend and provided several answer options. The 1986 version provided "less often [than several times a year]" as the least frequent option; the 2002 version added "never" as an answer option. The effect may have been to suggest to the 2002 interviewees that saying "less often" was not so embarrassing or socially awkward an answer as "never" and

therefore was an appropriate choice (compare to the "frivisit" and "bstvisit" variables in the GSS).

35. Much of the speculation about the problematic nature of the 2004 GSS "important matters" probe centered on the fact that it came at the end of a series of intrusive questions, unlike the 1985 version (Fischer 2009; McPherson 2009).

36. For example, about every two weeks the Gallup Poll asks an identical question about how often respondents go to church. From January 2009 through November 2009, the percentage answering "never" varied from a low of fourteen in mid-May to a high of twenty-three in mid-November— a nine-point gap that would be considered a big social change if the two numbers had been reported for, say, a decade apart (see "Gallup Brain," available [by subscription only] at: http://institution.gallup.com/ [accessed December 14, 2009]).

37. These comments are based on my reading of *Public Opinion Quarterly.* See Keeter et al. (2007); Curtin, Presser, and Singer (2005); and Nate Silver, "Estimating the Cellphone Effect: 2.8 Points," *FiveThirtyEight,* available at: http://www.fivethirtyeight.com/2008/09/estimating-cellphone-effect-22-points.html (accessed December 14, 2009).

38. For example, the online database for the American National Election Survey codes *everyone* who was interviewed in 2002 as saying that they *never* discussed politics with anyone (variable "VCF0733"), even if the respondents were not asked the question.

39. Kessler (1992); Thoits (1995).

40. These are questions from the oft-used UCLA Loneliness Scale (Russell 1996); for examples of its extensive use, see Cacioppo and Patrick (2008).

41. See, for example, Russell (1996); Cutrona (1986); Dykstra, van Tilburg, and de Jong Gierveld (2005); Victor et al. (2005); and Cacioppo and Patrick (2008). John Cacioppo and William Patrick (2008, 13), in their popular book *Loneliness,* note that "at least among young adults, those who feel lonely actually spend no more time alone than do those who feel more connected."

42. This discussion draws from Fischer (2010, 192–94).

43. For overviews, see Smith (1997), Uslaner (2002), Putnam (2000, ch. 8), and Nannestad (2008). The longest series are from the American National Election Study (1964 on) and the General Social Survey (1972 on), both available online (see, for example, http://sda.berkeley.edu/) and both reported in many sources. The post-1960s numbers are from the ANES. Note that the ANES results show an upswing to 47 percent in the period 2000 to 2004, but some of that rise was due to occasional telephone interviews (Arthur Lupia, Institute for Social Research, personal communication, March 18, 2008). Holding the method constant, 45 percent is a better estimate. The GSS trend is more uniformly declining: about 43 percent trusting answers in the 1970s, 36 percent in the 1990s, and 33 percent in the period 2006 to 2008 (English

interviews only for comparability). The decline is largely a cohort rather than a period effect (Robinson and Jackson 2001; also my analysis).

44.   Putnam (2000, ch. 8); Rahn and Transue (1998). Eric Uslaner (2002, ch. 6) contends that rising inequality explains most of the decline.

45.   Aggregate results from the ANES trust series correlate –.64 with the homicide rate lagged four years (my analysis; see also Fischer 1981).

46.   Costa and Kahn (2003a, 2003b); Putnam (2007); Alesina and La Ferrara (2002). Uslaner (forthcoming) dissents.

47.   And some argue that too much has been made of one question. Russell Hardin concluded that scholars have learned virtually nothing from all this research (quoted in Nannestad 2008, 431).

48.   The journal *Public Opinion Quarterly* is largely devoted to these concerns. A few among the many books are Schuman (2008); Tourangeau, Rips, and Rasinski (2000); and Converse and Presser (1986).

49.   See, for example, Cacioppo and Patrick (2008, 52–53).

50.   U.S. Bureau of the Census, "Table HH-4: Households by Size: 1960 to Present," available at: http://www.census.gov/population/socdemo/hh-fam/hh4.xls (accessed October 20, 2009).

51.   The increase from 4 to 11 percent is from estimations using the table in note 50. The 15 percent figure is calculated from U.S. Bureau of the Census, "Table A2: Family Status and Household Relationship of People 15 Years and Over, by Marital Status, Age, and Sex: 2008," available at: http://www. census.gov/population/socdemo/hh-fam/cps2008/tabA2-all.xls (accessed October 20, 2009).

52.   Fischer and Hout (2006, 83–86).

53.   See, for example, Alwin, Converse, and Martin (1985); and Fischer and Phillips (1982).

54.   For a literature review on mobility, see Fischer (2000). In the GSS, for example, respondents who were no longer living in the same town they had lived in at age sixteen tended to list *more* confidants than those still living in their childhood communities. Using the GSS, I ran "numgiven" on "mobile16" ("When you were sixteen years old, were you living in this same [city/town/county]?") for the 1985 and 1987 versions of the "important matters" question, with and without controlling for (a quadratic function of) age. Those who said "yes" listed slightly but significantly fewer names than those who said "no," and it did not matter whether they were still in the original state or not. (The results for 2004 are similar.)

55.   In the GSS, the separated and divorced named as many confidants (the "important matters" item) as the married did. I regressed "numgiven" on dummies for the categories of the variable "marital," combining separated and divorced, for 1985, 1987, and 2004. There were no significant differences with or without controls for age (quadratic function)—and age generally explained away all marital status effects.

56. *Perceptions* of being unloved are correlated with thoughts of suicide, but not that overwhelmingly, and with measures more closely approximating actual network attributes yet more weakly (see, for example, Arria et al. 2009; Norlev et al. 2005).

57. In Fischer (2010, 233–34), I discuss trends and provide citations.

58. See, for example, Mollenhorst (2009).

59. A point I stress in Fischer (2005).

60. Putnam (2000, 93).

61. So, for example, the Roper survey database (Brady et al. 2000) contains many more items about friends and family than I use here. Most of them, however, were asked only over a short span of fewer than five years (and they cannot be easily, if at all, "stitched" together or "cross-walked"). It makes little sense to spend time on such short-term "trends" to learn about change between 1970 and 2010.

62. See University of Michigan, Inter-University Consortium for Political and Social Research, http://www.icpsr.umich.edu/icpsrweb/ICPSR/; Roper Center, Public Opinion Archives, http://www.ropercenter.uconn.edu/; Gallup Brain, http://institution.gallup.com/ (by subscription only); Polling the Nations, http://poll.orspub.com/; and World Values Survey, http://www.worldvaluessurvey.org/.

63. See General Social Survey, http://www.norc.org/GSS+Website/.

64. Brady et al. (2000).

65. Tests of statistical significance are important in many contexts, but they do not provide sufficient guidance here because they address only random "error" in sampling—that is, in whether the change between one year and another could have occurred by a fluke of sampling—and they do not provide estimates for the sorts of systematic errors introduced by any of the other disturbances discussed earlier, such as wording changes. Even setting such biases aside, it is also true that, with large enough samples, statistical significance can be attained for numerical differences that make little social difference.

Chapter 3

1. Calculated from U.S. Bureau of the Census, "Table MS-1: Marital Status of the Population 15 Years Old and Over, by Sex and Race: 1950 to Present," available at: http://www.census.gov/population/www/socdemo/hh-fam. html#history (accessed December 18, 2009). The published figures are for Americans age fifteen and older, but the differences cited in the text should be about right.

2. These are crude estimates, to be sure. In the period 2006 to 2008, the American Community Survey found that 5.4 percent of households, about 6.1 million, were "unmarried partner" households (U.S. Bureau of the Census, American FactFinder, "Table S1101: Households and Families,

2006–2008: American Community Survey Three-Year Estimates," http://factfinder.census.gov/[accessed September 19, 2010]). Taking those estimates to mean that about 12 million Americans lived in such arrangements, and then combining that with the marital status data used in the previous note, implies that about 54 percent of Americans in 2008 were married, but about 60 percent of Americans were in "unions" of marriage or cohabitation. For estimates of this trend, see Fischer and Hout (2006, 68–70). For these rough purposes we can assume that there were, in percentage terms, few cohabiting households in 1970.

3. See, for example, Thoits (1995) for references to the research that affirms the obvious.

4. U.S. Bureau of the Census, *Statistical Abstract 2010*, "Table 78: Live Births, Deaths, Marriages, and Divorces," available at: http://www.census.gov/compendia/statab/2010/tables/10s0078.xls (accessed September 19, 2010).

5. A fuller discussion of these trends appears in Fischer and Hout (2006, ch. 4).

6. "Simplify" in the sense of excluding respondents whose parents might still be having children and excluding the elderly, many of whose siblings might be deceased.

7. These statistics, as with virtually all other GSS analyses reported in this book, use the GSS weight "compwt" to estimate population numbers. The analysis was done using the online SDA package available through the University of California–Berkeley (http://sda.berkeley.edu/). The question is: "How many brothers and sisters did you have? Please count those born alive, but no longer living, as well as those alive now. Also include stepbrothers and stepsisters, and children adopted by your parents." The variable "sibs" has a long tail, with respondents offering as many as sixty-eight siblings. Recoding "eleven or more siblings" to "ten" yields means of about 0.1 less in each decade.

8. The GSS question labeled "childs": "How many children have you ever had? Please count all that were born alive at any time (including any you had from a previous marriage)." Looking only at respondents age fifty or older—who presumably were finished with childbearing—yields means of 2.7 and 2.6, a narrower gap because of the baby boom. In the 1980s, respondents over the age of fifty reported having ever had 2.9 children, reflecting that boom.

9. Calculated from Gallup items, via "Gallup Brain," and the GSS item "chldidel," which asked respondents what they thought was the "ideal number of children for a family to have." (I recoded answers of "more than seven" to "seven" for calculating means.) Note, however, that the percentage of GSS respondents who answered "as many as they want" rose from 6 to 12 percent.

10. U.S. Bureau of the Census, "Table HH-4: Households by Size: 1960 to Present," available at: http://www.census.gov/population/socdemo/hh-fam/hh4.xls (accessed February 18, 2010). Estimating the percentage in large households required a calculation in which I coded households of more

than seven people as seven people. Note that this percentage is of *people*, not of *households.*

11. I took the GSS estimates for siblings and children ever born, in the 1970s versus the 2000s, and roughly calculated what those numbers would have been for the *parents* of middle-aged respondents in the 1970s. I multiplied these numbers through to get an average of about thirty-five parents, aunts, uncles, siblings, cousins, children, nieces, and nephews per GSS respondent in the 1970s and about twenty-six per GSS respondent in the 2000s.

12. I calculated these rates from census data on the marital status of Americans age fifteen and older (U.S. Bureau of the Census, "Table MS-1: Marital Status of the Population 15 Years and Over, by Sex and Race: 1950 to Present," available at: http://www.census.gov/population/www/socdemo/hh-fam. html#history [accessed December 18, 2009]) and from estimates of the percentage of currently married Americans age eighteen and older who had once been divorced or separated, based on the GSS "divorce" variable. This obviously makes a crude fit, but I could not find remarriage data into the 2000s. The rough estimates are that, in 1970, 55 percent of people age fifteen and older were once married, 25 percent were never married, 8 percent were widowed, 3 percent were divorced—and about 9 percent were married but had once been divorced. For 2008 the figures are 41 percent once married, 30 percent never married, 6 percent widowed, 10 percent divorced, and 14 percent remarried.

13. For an overview, see Swartz (2009).

14. Gillis (1996).

15. In brief, the sample is based on fewer than 5 percent of persons who appeared on a list of target households provided by commercial brokers. The 5 percent agreed to be part of a regular panel of respondents to mail surveys. Putnam (2000, 420–24) discusses the specifics in great detail in *Bowling Alone.* See also a comparative test by Pollard (n.d.) and Keum et al. (2004), another example of a use of this mail survey.

16. Putnam (2000, 101).

17. Putnam focuses on the percentage who "definitely agree" with the statement—dividing the responses that way shows the most dramatic decline. I use the total who agree to any degree because that is all that is provided in the published 1998 to 2003 results. Using the total sample before 1985 makes no sense because in those years DDB Needham effectively sampled only married people. And the answers to the question make sense only for the subset of respondents who lived in multi-person households. Costa and Kahn (2003a) analyze this item and focus on married twenty-five- to fifty-four-year-olds. Putnam reports on—and I also analyzed—another question that DDB asked respondents to agree or disagree with: "We usually have a large family breakfast on weekends." The trends are similar.

18. The Roper data on family activities are, on the one hand, an unusually consistent series of questions over a few decades. On the other hand, they

are beset by (apparent) changes in sample, sponsor, number of questions, unknown methodological decisions, and ambiguous documentation. The only systematic set of Roper family activities data are for 1976, 1986, and 1990, compiled by Brady et al. (2000). Unfortunately, the 1976 questions are only for parents of children ages seven to seventeen (it appears). Moreover, data after 1994 are not in the public domain and thus are impossible or prohibitively expensive to see (Marilyn Milliken, Roper Center, personal communication, February 26, 2010). Putnam (2000, 101) presents a selected set of results from 1997. The guide to the Roper family activities data, by year, is as follows: 1974—poll conducted for Virginia Slims (weighted toward women, but I have averaged male and female answers to get national estimates), from iPoll, USROPER.74VASL; 1976—regular Roper poll, from Brady et al. (2000) (family questions asked only of parents of seven- to seventeen-year-olds); 1982—poll conducted for Television Information Office, from iPoll, USROPER.040083; 1986—regular Roper poll, from Brady et al. (2000) (the Brady codebook states that the family questions were asked of all parents, but the iPoll reports say they were asked only of parents of seven- to seventeen-year-olds [iPoll USROPER.86-6]); 1990—regular Roper poll, from Brady et al. (2000) (the family questions were asked only of parents of under-eighteen-year olds); 1991—poll conducted for *Good Housekeeping* (women only), iPoll, USROPER.91GOOD (the iPoll records do not stipulate that the question was addressed to parents of children under eighteen, but that seems a fair assumption); 1994—poll conducted for the Network Television Association by Roper Starch Worldwide, from iPoll, USROPER.94TV; 1997—results cited by Putnam (2000, 101).

19. Using the 1976, 1980, and 1990 data, I ran a logit model with "frequently" ate the main meal together as the dependent variable. I pooled all parents into this sample, but included controls for having children under age thirteen and having children ages thirteen to seventeen or eighteen. The contrast of 1986 and 1990 with 1976 remained significant and substantial—e^b = .6 and .7 for 1986 and 1990 after controls. Fathers, blacks, and parents of teens were the *least* likely to say that the family "frequently" ate meals together.

20. Suzanne Bianchi, John Robinson, and Melissa Milkie (2006, 153) report a modest decline in the time-budget studies they analyze. Paul Amato and his colleagues (2007, fig. 2.3) report a drop in the proportion of spouses who say they "almost always" have the main meal together, from 78 percent in 1980 to 66 percent in 2000. They also report sizable declines in "almost always" answers for other joint spousal activities, such as visiting friends together (down from 53 to 34 percent).

21. AP-iVillage poll, conducted by GfK Roper Public Affairs & Media, GfK Custom Research, available at: http://www.ap-gfkpoll.com/(accessed November 13, 2009).

22. A Shell Oil Company–sponsored survey (in the Polling the Nations database) asked, "I'm going to mention a few practices or places, and for each one, please tell me whether you think it will still exist in America thirty years from now, or whether you think it will have pretty much disappeared: families sitting down to eat dinner together." Forty-nine percent said that fami-

lies eating dinner together would still exist in thirty years, and 47 percent said that the practice would disappear.

23. A series of surveys done of teens age twelve to seventeen shows little change in the 2000s. Asked, "In a typical week, how often do you and your parents [or guardian] eat dinner together?" 41 percent in 2000 said "seven times," and 40 percent in 2006 gave this answer; surveys by the National Center on Addiction and Substance Abuse at Columbia University, reported in Polling the Nations. These and other data suggest that the drop depicted in figures 3.1 to 3.4 may well have flattened out after the 1990s.

24. While the 1976, 1986, and 1990 polls were part of Roper's regular polling, the 1994 one was done for a television organization and, among other things, had a different lineup of activities. See the notes to figure 3.5.

25. A logit model on the 1976, 1986, and 1990 samples with the answer that the family "frequently" or "often" ate out together as the dependent variable showed the year effect to be persistent, after controls, at $e^b = 1.5$ and 2.0 for 1986 and 1990. (The fully employed, mothers, and nonblacks were especially likely to say "frequently" or "often.")

26. A pair of mid-1990s Wirthlin polls treat similar topics, but their answer categories differ from one another.

27. In their comparison of survey respondents' time-budgets in 2000 to those conducted in each of the previous four decades, Bianchi and her colleagues (2006) report more parent-child time together in 2000. The trend continued to at least 2003 (Bianchi 2007; Bianchi, personal communication, December 30, 2009). Garey Ramey and Valeries Ramey (2010) show the upward trend accelerating in the mid-2000s. See also Hofferth and Sandberg (2001) and Sandberg and Hofferth (2005).

28. In the 1974 poll, 28 percent of all parents said they frequently did food shopping as a family; in 1986, 31 percent did; and in 1990, 41 percent did. Parents with only teenagers at home reported rates of food shopping as a family of 20, 26, and 33 percent for 1976, 1980, and 1990. It appears that Roper did not ask the shopping item after 1990.

29. Bahr et al. (2004). Unfortunately, a procedural change between the two years and a shift in the demographic composition of the students may have affected this result. Ramey and Ramey (2010) found that increased time with parents was true for older, not younger, children.

30. Gallup Brain, "End of the '80s" survey, December 1987: "Among your friends and the people you know, do you think the following are gaining favor and popularity or are losing favor and popularity . . . Parents spending more time with their children?" Twenty-seven percent said "losing."

31. Amato et al. (2007); Bianchi, Robinson, and Milkie (2006, 104).

32. I categorized the few fathers whose whereabouts were unknown to respondents as "never" seen.

33. Many studies have found that respondents are more willing to report drug use, abortions, and potentially embarrassing sexual behavior on some form

of SAQ than directly to an interviewer (Tourangeau and Smith 1996, especially table 1). A few studies, however, find only modest differences (Krysan 1998; Aquilino 1994; compare Bishop and Fisher 1995).

34. Another methodological difference is that the 2002 version offers respondents a "never" option, while the 1986 one offered "less often [than several times a year]" as the lowest option. Standard survey wisdom suggests that this difference would nudge 2002 respondents downward.

35. Of the respondents in 1986 whose fathers were alive, 18 percent had lived apart from those fathers at age sixteen (GSS variable "family16"), while 29 percent of similar 2002 respondents had lived apart from their fathers. Logit analyses of the mother visit variable (weekly visits or more) showed nonsignificant effects for 2002 versus 1986. Frequent visitors lived near their mothers, tended to be women, and never married. Logit analyses for seeing fathers weekly or more also yielded nonsignificant year effects (zero-order or after controls). Reports of frequent visits tended to come from respondents who had at age sixteen lived with their fathers, were less educated, widowed, younger, and had infants in their homes. (The GSS did not ask how far away fathers lived.) See Swartz (2009, 194) for further data on frequency of contact with parents.

36. In 1986 and 1994, GSS respondents answered the "social evening" questions and also answered the questions displayed in figure 3.12 about how often they saw their mothers and fathers. The answers to the "social evening" and "parent-visiting" questions were highly correlated, which gives us some confidence about using the "social evening" questions to measure face-to-face contact. Setting aside parents who shared a household with the respondent, the associations were: (a) mavisit × socpars, 1986, gamma = .75; (b) mavisit × socpars, 1994, gamma = .77; and (c) pavisit × socpars, 1986, gamma = .63. In 1986 the GSS also asked respondents how often they had seen a brother or a sister. The association between those items and the "socsibs" item were: (d) brovisit × socsibs, gamma = .56; (e) sisvisit × socsibs, gamma = .65. Given that the behaviors asked about are only roughly equivalent—for example, you could see your mother daily but never for a social evening, or you could join "a brother or sister" often for a social evening but really mean only your sister—these are strong associations. By the way, the 1986 "how often do you see your sister/brother" question was never repeated in the same format.

37. These nontrends are robust to controls; there appears to have been little change over the years. Restricting the sample to respondents age twenty-five through fifty-four—in order to minimize the effects of respondents being dependents of their parents or having especially elderly parents—makes no difference to the trends shown in the figure. I also checked on the possible effect of adding Spanish-language interviews in the later years: negligible. Regression analyses, with controls, using the full response scales (rather than logits for several times a month), yield no significant effects for year—except a small, positive one for the "relatives" item (beta = .05). Reports of spending frequent social evenings with any of these categories of relatives were

more common for women, nonwhites, and the less educated. In addition, the unmarried and younger respondents reported more frequently spending evenings with parents and siblings, while the middle-aged and ever-married reported spending more evenings with "relatives," presumably because that category included in-laws. Finally, Peter Marsden and Sameer Srivastava (2011) analyzed these data using many controls and testing age-period-cohort effects. They found only a small, residual, late, upward period trend in the "relatives" item.

38. Survey conducted for the Anti-Defamation League of the B'nai B'rith by the National Opinion Research Center (the polling organization for the GSS) and archived by the Roper Center's iPoll, USNORC.64BNAI.R48A.

39. For respondents living an hour or more away, the percentage having contact several times a week or more rose from 10 to 23 percent.

40. In logit regressions of the dependent variables—weekly or more frequent contact with mothers/fathers—the 2002 versus 1986 effect is either marginally significant (positive for mothers) or not significant. Across the two years, reports of frequent contact with mothers were greatest for those living closer, younger respondents, women, and the more educated; with fathers, it was greatest for those who at age sixteen had lived with their father and those who were younger. (Distance was not available in 2002 for fathers.)

41. The question was: "How often do you talk on the phone or get together with relatives who do not live with you—most every day, a few times a week, a few times a month, about once a month, or less than once a month?" The percentage of eighteen- to fifty-four-year-olds saying "at least a few times a week" was about 47 each time. (The first survey covered only those ages, so I compared them to eighteen- to fifty-four-year-olds in the second survey.) (National Comorbidity Survey: Baseline [NCS-1], 1990–1992, obtained from University of Michigan, Inter-University Consortium for Political and Social Research [ICPSR], study 6693; and National Comorbidity Survey Replication [NCS-R], 2001–2003, ICPSR study 189.)

42. This conclusion is consistent with Costa and Kahn's (2003a) analysis. Putnam (2000) dismisses the working-wife explanation (although he does argue that longer job commutes were a factor in the declining social life he described). Putnam bases his dismissal on the fact that many of the trends he reported held for nonworking women as well as for employed ones. However, that logic ignores the network or collective effect of working women.

Chapter 4

1. On social contexts (or, as Scott Feld has termed them, social foci), see Fischer (1982a, 79ff.), Feld (1981), and Mollenhorst (2009).

2. Around 1970, 30 percent of eighteen- to twenty-four-year olds were in high school or college (26 percent in college); in 2007, 45 percent were in high school or college (39 percent in college). Meanwhile, the high school dropout

rate slumped from about 17 percent to 10 percent (calculated from U.S. Bureau of the Census, Historical Tables A-5a and A-5b, available at: http://www.census.gov/population/www/socdemo/school.html [accessed December 16, 2009]).

3. From Current Population Survey (CPS), Survey Series ID LNU01300025Q and LNU01300026Q, via U.S. Bureau of Labor Statistics databases, http://www.bls.gov/data/ (accessed December 15, 2009).

4. The GSS "attend" item shows that about 21 percent of respondents in the 1970s said that they never attended services or did so less than once a year, and about 27 percent in the 2000s said they never did. Data from the American National Election Study (ANES) are more complex, because question wording changed over time, but an estimate, adjusting for that, would be that the non-attenders rose from about 19 percent in the 1970s to about 25 percent in the 2000s (items "vcf0130a," "v083185," and "v083186"). For a fuller discussion of this topic, see Fischer and Hout (2006, ch. 8).

5. From GSS item "sunsch16"; cohort comparisons.

6. The GSS "nummem" variable is the main measure that scholars have used. In the 1970s, 27 percent of respondents claimed *no* memberships out of a list of over a dozen types of organizations listed for them by interviewers. In the 1980s, 31 percent claimed no such memberships, and in the early 1990s, 30 percent did. The GSS ceased asking the question for several years. The last available estimate is 38 percent claiming no memberships for 2004. (Critics complain that the list has stayed the same, while the nature of Americans' memberships has changed.) Interestingly, there seemed to be no decline in *multiple* memberships among those with at least one. Robert Putnam's papers on civic engagement in the mid-1990s, as well as his *Bowling Alone*, stirred a fierce debate on this issue that I do not review here.

7. In 2000 and 2002, the GSS asked people who had said they used a computer an hour or more a week for more than simply email: "Have you ever first come into contact with someone on the Internet—through a chat room, bulletin board, news group, discussion forum, or other interactive site, or through their Web page—with whom you later established a relationship outside the Internet?" Of these Internet users, about 10 percent said "yes" each year. My rough calculations are that this translates into about 2 percent of all the survey respondents, although that may be a low estimate even for 2001.

8. Calculated from analysis of Pew Internet and American Life Project, "September 2005—Online Dating" (December 8, 2005), available at: http://www.pewinternet.org/Shared-Content/Data-Sets/2005/September-2005—Online-Dating.aspx (accessed December 17, 2009).

9. Hampton, Sessions, and Her (2009, 36–37).

10. In 2004 about 30 percent of Internet users surveyed by Pew claimed that it had expanded their "core" and casual ties, while about 2 percent said that it had reduced their ties (Rainie et al. 2006). Statistical analysis of the respon-

dents' answers suggests a modest expansion of "significant," if not "core," ties. Keith Hampton reports a strong independent association of Internet use with network size (Hampton, Sessions, and Her 2009, tables D-8 and D-9, as *amended* in personal communication, January 5, 2010).

11. Based on logit equations with GSS item "peocntct." Work and school status, education, and race are overwhelmingly the strongest predictors of high numbers. Working full-time increased the odds of reporting many contacts about fivefold compared to those not working or attending school.

12. In the GSS samples, the percentage of women with jobs or going to school (variable labeled "wrkstat") rose from about 42 percent to 64 percent from the early 1970s to the mid-2000s; the percentage for men showed virtually no change, holding steady at about 77 percent.

13. The average journey to work in the United States rose from 21.7 minutes in 1980 to 22.4 minutes in 1990, 25.5 minutes in 2000, and 25.3 minutes in 2007 (Reschovsky 2004, table 2; U.S. Bureau of the Census, "Travel Time to Work for the United States: 1990 and 1980 Census," available at: http://www.census.gov/population/socdemo/journey/ustime.txt [accessed July 19, 2010]; and U.S. Bureau of the Census, American FactFinder, "Table S0801: 2006–2008 American Community Survey Three-Year Estimates," available at: http://factfinder.census.gov/home/saff/main.html?_lang=en [accessed July 19, 2010]).

14. Ideally, the GSS "numgiven" question—"Who do you discuss important matters with?"—asked in 1985 and 2004, might have provided one indicator, but as I discussed in chapter 1, the 2004 replication is probably flawed. Also, the single question may tap an important dimension of social ties, but it is only a single dimension (Rainie and Wellmann 2011).

15. I collapsed answers of six through as many as ninety close friends because the high numbers are extremely variable.

16. In the Gallup series, used in figure 4.1, those who reported no close friends varied from 3 percent in 1976 and 1990 to 2 percent in the 2000s. The GSS has used more diverse questions to count friendship. In answer to the question used for figure 4.2, 9 percent claimed to have no friends in 1998 and 4 percent did so in 2002. The questions used for figure 4.3 asked respondents to *name*—not just count—a few "good friends" to whom they "feel close" (other than their spouse). In 1988, 3 percent offered "none," and 5 percent said "none" in 1998. (Explicit variables for these figure 4.3 questions do not appear in the 1988 or 1998 GSS surveys. I had to construct them from a series designed to determine whether respondents had good friends in their church congregations.) A 1975 survey was similar to this GSS series in asking respondents to write down the names of "good friends" who were not immediate family. In that survey, 5 percent said they had no good friends— effectively the same percentage (Jackman and Jackman 1983, 173; the median number of friends that respondents listed was six). The Saguaro questions used for figure 4.4 asked respondents, "About how many close friends do you have these days? These are people you feel at ease with, can talk to about

private matters, or call on for help. Would you say that you have no close friends, one or two, three to five, six to ten, or more than that?" In each of the three recent years, 4 percent said they had no close friends.

Another couple of data points address—not the trend—but the level of friendlessness circa 2004. In 2000 through 2004, the GSS asked, "Not counting people at work or family at home, about how many other friends or relatives do you keep in contact with at least once a year?" (variable labeled "numcntct"). This question does not refer to "close friends," of course, but is still informative. Two percent said "none." In 2008 the Pew Research Center asked respondents in a telephone survey the same "numgiven" question that McPherson, Smith-Lovin, and Brashears (2006, 2009) used and did find a two-digit result: 12 percent reported that they had no one to discuss "important matters" with (Hampton, Sessions, and Her 2009)—about half of the estimate of McPherson and his colleagues (2009).

17. Amato et al. (2007, 178ff.).

18. Wang and Wellman (2010, table 2).

19. The striking consensus here of low percentages and no trends makes the "finding" of McPherson and his colleagues (2009) that about one-fourth or one-fifth of Americans in 2004, up from about one-twelfth in 1985, were without any confidants (kin *or* nonkin) all the more anomalous.

20. Figure 4.1, the Gallup series, might suggest that fewer Americans reported having six or more close friends after 1976, but as I noted, the 1976 point includes fifteen- to seventeen-year-olds. Figure 4.2 would suggest a twenty-first-century surge in friendships, but the 2002 point in that figure is distorted because it is based on a more intensive set of questions than the earlier points. However, the 1988 and 1998 GSS questions displayed in figure 4.3, asking respondents to name a few good friends, does show a nine-point decline in the percentage who named three or more "good friends." (There is a potential methodological issue here. The 1998 version accepted up to five names while the 1988 version accepted up to three. Interviewers were encouraged to ask respondents if there were any more names they could add. One might imagine that five blank spaces rather than three would have led the 1998 interviewers to extract more names from respondents who initially gave only one or two names than the 1988 interviewers would have extracted. If so—and this is simply speculation—the bias would have led to actually underestimating the shrinkage in networks.) Figure 4.4 shows essentially no change during the early 2000s.

21. Amato et al. (2007, 178ff.).

22. Wang and Wellman (2010, table 2). The studies using estimated numbers, such as this one and Amato et al. (2007), get sometimes puzzling results because of skewed distributions. For example, among heavy Internet users in the Wang and Wellman sample, the mean number of "off-line" friends went up a lot, but the median went down.

23. Amato et al. (2007, 183). Note that the upper age here was fifty-five.

24. Wang and Wellman (2010).

25. With respect to who was totally friendless, the cohort patterns for figure 4.2 are inconsistent. With respect to the number of friends, two of the three surveys suggested a decline from earlier to later generations. In 1986 respondents born before 1931 more often reported themselves as friendless than did respondents born later; in 1998 more baby boomers claimed to have no friends than did those born before or after; in 2002 there was no difference. In 1986 and 1998, the more recently born respondents were less likely to report having six or more friends; in 2002 there was no difference by cohort. In figure 4.3, the results from the 1988 and 1998 surveys that asked respondents to name close friends suggest that it was the *earliest* born—those born before 1931—who tended to have the smallest networks. This is mixed evidence, but perhaps leans in the direction of more recent cohorts being a bit less likely to claim *many* friends. Trying to separate out period-age-cohort effects is a perennial bramble for social scientists.

26. As with the GSS parents questions discussed earlier, the 1986 item was administered face-to-face and the 2002 version in an SAQ. The year difference persists in logit equations with controls predicting whether the respondent saw the best friend at least weekly; the only other significant predictors of frequent visiting are being less educated and having never been married. Unlike the parallel question about seeing one's mother, we have no measure of distance.

27. Putnam (2000, 458, note 15).

28. I analyzed only the 1985 panel because in 1987 and 2004, the GSS did not ask the "social evening" questions of the same respondents who received the "important matters" question. Respondents who in 1985 reported spending several social evenings a month with friends outside the neighborhood averaged 1.6 nonkin associates in answer to the "important matters" question, compared to 1.2 nonkin for those who reported spending fewer such evenings. In fuller analyses, I regressed the full variable labeled "numgiven" on the entire set of "social evening" questions (relatives, neighbors, friends) and going out to a bar, controlling for age, sex, race, being married, and education. In the reduced equation (R^2 = .18), reporting more evenings spent with relatives remains a predictor of listing more names. So does reporting more social evenings spent with friends (with the exception of those who said that they spent such evenings "almost daily"—these respondents listed slightly fewer names). But never spending an evening with a neighbor is also a predictor of listing more names; those who seemed to ignore their neighbors had larger networks. If one counts only the number of nonkin respondents named in the "numgiven" item as the dependent variable, then reports of more frequent social evenings spent with friends or with neighbors will predict more names, while reports of evenings more frequently spent with relatives will predict fewer names; going to bars makes no difference (R^2, with controls = .13). In sum, the "social evening" questions seem to tap nonkin networks.

29. The "social evening" item correlates with, in the 2002 survey, respondents estimating higher numbers of persons with whom they were in annual contact and, in 1986 and 1992, with estimating a higher number of friends. (Cross-tabulating "socfrend" with: "numcntct" in 2002, gamma = .15; "frinum" in 1986, gamma = .15; "numfrend" in 1998, gamma = .09. Replicators should note that I made sure there was a zero value coded for each of the count variables.) Inspection of the tables shows that the respondents who estimated no friends or very few friends or contacts tended also to be the ones who rarely spent a social evening with friends. There is much weaker association at the higher levels: respondents with many friends were not especially more likely to report spending many evenings out with friends than were respondents with an average number of friends.

30. In OLS regressions of the entire "socfrend" scale for all the years (n > 30,000), with controls, year is not significant. Frequent socializers tend to be young, never-married, childless, educated, and white. Marsden and Srivastava's (2011) much fuller analysis of this item concludes that there is essentially a negligible time trend.

31. Regarding the 1964 point, see note 38, chapter 3.

32. In OLS regressions of the entire "soccommun" scale for all the surveys, year remains a significant predictor after controls. Respondents who reported spending more social evenings with neighbors tended to be younger, never-married, without infants at home, more educated, residents of small communities, and not working (especially women who were not working). Avery Guest and Susan Wierzbicki (1999) noted the divergence of the two items early on. Marsden and Srivastava's (2011) extensive analysis concludes that, ceteris paribus, there is a negative effect of year, but—surprisingly—a positive effect of cohort on the "neighbors" item.

33. If there is any substantive trend, it is toward an increase in *moderate* levels of bar-going; both reports of high rates and of not going at all declined modestly. Marsden and Srivastava (2011) found a small, negative independent effect of year on bar visiting, but a small, positive independent effect of cohort.

34. The question is: "Thinking again about yesterday . . . did you . . . visit with family or friends?" The surveys were conducted by PSRA for the Times Mirror Company in 1994 and 1995 and then for the Pew Research Center. Although additional polls used this question, the five most comparable surveys show 57 percent answering "yes" in 1994 and 66 percent in 2000. See Roper Center, iPoll, USPSRA.052494.R11G, USPSRA.101695.R011B, USPSRA.97006.Q17C, USPSRA.98JUN8.R15F, USPSRA.00ONLM.R26B.

35. In the 1985 to 1998 segment of the data (the later data are not available for reanalysis), year is associated with the full "visfrd" one-to-six scale at beta = −.02, which is statistically significant given a sample of over 50,000, but is substantively trivial. With controls for age, sex, education, being married, and having children at home, again beta = −.02. (From 1979 to 1998, among respondents in households with at least two residents, the zero-order beta = −.01, and the partial beta is −.02.)

36. This is a robust trend that survives various sorts of controls. See also the analyses by Putnam (2000) and Costa and Kahn (2003a).

37. Among respondents in households with at least two residents, the percentage who ever gave or attended a dinner party in the previous twelve months dropped from about 80 percent around 1980 to about 70 percent at the end of the century. The percentage of those who had at least five such events dropped from about 50 percent to 30 percent.

38. The year effect is highly significant and robust after controls, $e^b = .96$. Going to friends' homes was especially common among younger respondents, those who were more educated, and those without young children at home.

39. Along those lines, answers to a Saguaro question—"About how often do you talk to or visit with your immediate neighbors?"—show a small decline, from 53 percent saying "just about every day" in 2000 to 48 percent saying that in 2006. Assuming that this "talk or visit" occurs in or around the home makes the trend consistent with other items on at-home social activity (survey conducted by the Saguaro Seminar: Civic Engagement in America at John F. Kennedy School of Government, Harvard University, available at: www.ksg.harvard.edu/saguaro (accessed November 12, 2010); obtained via iPoll: USSAGS.00SOCC.Q51, USSAGS.06SOCC.Q51).

40. Putnam (2000, 99); Veroff, Douvan, and Kulka (1981, 479–80).

41. This summary is based on analyses of largely the same time-budget surveys by Robinson and Godbey (1999), Bianchi, Robinson, and Milkie (2006), and Aguiar and Hurst (2007); see also NPD Group (1999). Part of the difficulty in drawing firm conclusions is that the procedures changed over the major time-budget studies in 1965, 1975, 1985, 1995, and 2000. Some of the greatest procedural changes affect comparisons of 1965 to later years; results from the 1965 survey were especially different from the later ones. Bianchi and her colleagues (2006) make the distinction between "visiting" as a "primary activity" and being "with" friends and relatives. So, for example, between 1975 and 2000, married fathers spent 23 percent less time on average "visiting" friends and relatives, but only 4 percent less time "with" friends and relatives. For married mothers, there was no change in "visiting" between 1975 and 2000, but a 9 percent drop in hours "with" friends and relatives (Bianchi, Robinson, and Milkie 2006, compare tables 5.3 and 5.7).

42. The difference remains nonsignificant in a logit analysis. Women were about 50 percent likelier, and the never-married about twice as likely, ceteris paribus, to have spoken weekly. The GSS did not ask about the distances between the respondents and their friends, and so we cannot take that into account.

43. A 2009 variation reported by Pew (not shown; available at Polling the Nations) asked, "In the past twenty-four hours, did you talk with family or friends, or not?" Overall, 93 percent said "yes."

44. On long-distance charges, see Noll (1994). In the Roper data on letter-writing, the year trend is not significant, despite an n over 25,000. In a full logit equation, year is significant but trivial, with $e^b = .99$; the major predictors of

letter writing are being female, educated, not black, and older. With respect to long-distance calling, the year effect remains strong, $e^b = 1.06$, with other major predictors being education, being female, married, employed full-time, and older.

45. The year effect is noteworthy before and after controls, $e^b = 1.03$ and 1.025. The major predictors of whether respondents "called off" this item from the list of activities are education, full-time employment, ever being married, being female, and being Hispanic or Asian. Potential users of these data should note that the computer file label for this variable, "paphone," reads, "Has respondent made a personal long-distance call in the last week?" but the codebook shows that the actual item does *not* include the word "personal."

46. The DDB data, although they provide many items, have little on social contact other than in-person contact among family and friends. There is only one extended series close to this topic: how often respondents sent greeting cards. There was trivial change over time in how often respondents reported having "sent a greeting card" in the previous twelve months. Are we surprised, by the way, that there is a major gender difference? Married men were the least likely to send greeting cards—about one in five sent twelve or more a year—while married women were the most likely to send greeting cards—about three in five did.

47. Bearman and Parigi (2004); Bailey and Marsden (1999).

48. Because, as of this writing, the 2008 ANES survey had not yet been merged with the full series, these models run only through 2004. I ran a logit regression, 1984 to 2004, for "vcf0731"—yes, does discuss politics—controlling for, after reducing larger equations, age, age-squared, education, sex, race (white), being married, and also the respondent's interest in politics ("vcf0313") and whether the respondent tried to persuade others how to vote ("vcf0717"). The e^b for year is 1.3 ($p < .001$). I also ran an OLS regression, 1984 to 2004, of how many days in the prior week the respondent had discussed politics, controlling for age, education, sex, race (white), being married, having never been married, and also interest in politics ("vcf0313") and whether the respondent tried to persuade others how to vote ("vcf0717"). The partial beta for year is .04 ($p < .001$) and for the year 2000 as a dummy, .30 ($p < .001$). (The effect of being female in both equations shifted from slightly negative to slightly positive after controlling for the two measures of respondents' interest in politics, which is consistent with the tendencies for women to be less interested in politics but more interested in talking to friends and relatives.) Answers to a related question in the World Values Survey—question A062, "When you get together with your friends, would you say you discuss political matters frequently, occasionally, or never?"—show a modest increase from 1982 to 1999 in those who say they "frequently" discuss politics, from 11 to 17 percent, and a decrease in those who "never" discuss politics, from 34 to 25 percent.

49. I ran a logit regression, 1972 to 2004, for "vcf0717" (respondent tried to persuade others how to vote), controlling for age, age-squared, sex, race, education, and being married, and also for "vcf0313" (how interested the respondent was in politics). The e^b for year is 1.1 ($p < .001$). The year 2008 was not in these regressions because the survey data for that year had not yet been integrated into the full ANES online data.

50. I consulted Henry Brady and Laurel Elm, experts on the Roper series.

51. There are several reasons for greater faith in the ANES: the ANES is held to higher academic standards for sampling, question construction, and data handling; the ANES data are much richer in political items setting the context for these questions; the ANES data cover a much longer duration; and the ANES data are continuously scoured by scholars, while the Roper data are relatively hard to access and use. (Only since Henry Brady and his colleagues [2000] compiled them have the social science data in the Roper polls been easily accessible, and that set runs only through 1994.) Moreover, the Roper item here is buried among about two dozen other activities in which respondents might have engaged in the prior week, such as buying yogurt and asking for a smoking-free section of a restaurant (presumably part of Roper's commercial work), items that shifted from year to year. (The iPoll archive at the Roper Center has the full texts and results only for the 1980 and 1984 polls. Brady and his colleagues [2000] extracted only the responses of social science interest.)

52. By Peter Marsden.

53. See notes 48 and 49 on statistical analyses of the ANES that suggest by controlling for political interest the same conclusion.

Chapter 5

1. Pescosolido et al. (2010); Swindle et al. (2000, table 1).

2. See World Values Survey, http://www.worldvaluessurvey.org/ (accessed January 12, 2010). Apparently, these questions were not asked in the last WVS wave in 2005.

3. GSS item "aged."

4. Daphna Gans and Merril Silverstein (2006) examined expressions of filial loyalty in the Los Angeles Study of Generations and, in a multivariate model, report a negative period effect of the 1990s versus the 1980s in such expression, but a major increase from earlier to later cohorts. Given the complexities of the model, the net trend is unclear. For discussion of Americans' familism, see Fischer (2010, ch. 4). For some data, see Fischer (2000).

5. See Ikkink, van Tilburg, and Knipscheer (1999); Arling (1987); Silverstein, Gans, and Yang (2006); Silverstein, Parrott, and Bengtson (1995); Schoeni and Ross (2005); McGarry and Schoeni (1997); and Robinson and Schoeni (2010), from which the 2005 survey statistics are drawn. The 2007 survey is Gallup's "Elder Care" poll, available from Gallup Brain: 11 percent of American

adults said that they were providing financial aid to at least one parent; 37 percent said that they were giving personal assistance, such as physical care or help around the home; and another 37 percent expected to provide one or the other kind of help in the future.

6. Robert F. Schoeni (personal communication, January 14, 2010) notes that the Panel Study of Income Dynamics (PSID) data on such transfers are clearly unreliable. Clark and Kenney (2010, table 2) use the Health and Retirement Survey and find that the probability that parents lent money to their adult children rose in the 1990s and then declined. A 2005 Pew survey compared reports of helping—gifts, practical help, and money—between 41-to-59-year-olds and their parents to similar results from a 1989 Gallup Poll and found minor differences (Pew Research Center 2005, 13).

7. Swartz (2009).

8. I also coded no check-offs—blank replies—as if the respondent had checked "no one."

9. The 1986 list of relatives reads: "spouse, mother, father, daughter, son, sister, brother, other relative," and the 2002 list reads "husband/wife/partner, mother, father, daughter, daughter-in-law, son, son-in-law, sister, brother, other blood relative, other in-law relative." Also, as the lists show, the 2002 version explicitly included "partner" as a synonym for "spouse"; some respondents in 1986 probably checked off unmarried partners as "friends." There were some other differences as well; see the notes to figure 5.1.

10. In a logit analysis combining 1986 and 2002, with the dependent variable being "failed to name two personal helpers if sick," year remains nonsignificant with several controls. This response was more common among older, male, and especially unmarried respondents.

11. It is possible that between 1986 and 2002 small loans became less accessible to Americans. Between those two years, the number of FDIC-insured community banks dropped from 5.7 to 2.7 per 1,000 Americans (Critchfield et al. 2005). This was part of an "unprecedented transformation" in the banking industry "marked by a substantial decline in the number of commercial banks and savings institutions and by a growing concentration of industry assets among a few dozen extremely large financial institutions" (Jones and Critchfield 2006). The James Stewart–like local banker was harder and harder to find. On the other hand, per capita loans to individuals by commercial banks and savings and loans institutions combined stayed about the same—about $2,700 (in 2002 dollars) in each year. An increasing portion of the loans took the form of credit card debts, which we can assume were running balances. Excluding that, per capita loans declined from about $2,000 to about $1,550, noteworthy but still not of the magnitude we would expect given the GSS results (Federal Deposit Insurance Corporation, "Historical Statistics on Banking (HSOB)," tables CB13 and S16, available at: http://www2.fdic.gov/hsob [accessed September 19, 2010]).

12. Logit regressions with controls do not change these year (non-)effects.

13. A few surveys have repeated questions about respondents providing help to others. (There are many surveys of respondents' help to their elderly parents, but none I found that were nationally representative and repeated.) Gallup asked variations of this question, as in this one from November 1989: "During the past twelve months, did you give money, food, or clothing to any of the following types of people?" In March 1990 the wording changed to "did you or members of your family or household . . . ," and in May 1996 it changed again, to "any of the following types of people in 1995." In February 1996 the GSS repeated the Gallup's 1990 version. If we just compare the identical wording across "houses," Gallup 1990 to GSS 1996, it would appear that the proportion helping "a needy relative" or "a needy friend" dropped sharply, while the percentage helping a "needy neighbor" rose slightly. If we compare just Gallup, irrespective of precise wording, we can only compare answers for "needy neighbor": 50, 40, and 30 percent, respectively, across 1989, 1990, and 1996. What to make of this is unclear, since giving is at least as much a function of the recipient's need as of the donor's social involvement (GSS items "needynei," "needyrel", "needyfrd"; Gallup, via the Roper Center iPoll, USGALLUP.112089.R08B/C/D, USGALLUP.90VOL.R042B/C/D, USGALLUP.96GIVE.Q032A/C).

14. In 1986, 9 percent of respondents checked "clergy," while in 2002 less than half of a percent checked "priest or member of the clergy." The size of the change and the wording differences make me skeptical that this is a real development.

15. On the methodological side, the 1986 survey offered one fewer relative category and one more friend category than the 2002 version ("closest friend" and "other friend" versus only "close friend"). On the substantive side, there is a detectable increase from 1986 to 2002 in the percentage of respondents, especially among the unmarried, who checked "mother," "father," "sister," or "brother."

16. Logit equations with the usual sets of controls do not change the conclusions about the zero-order trends discussed in this paragraph.

17. Two technical issues: (1) In both years, the National Comorbidity Studies followed up the question about how often the respondents let their spouse know about their worries ("v245" and "SN12") with a potentially useful question ("v246" and "SN13"): the unmarried respondents were simply asked directly how often they would let anyone know about their worries, and the married how often they would let anyone *else* (besides the spouse) know. The results show a dramatic drop over time in the percentage of the unmarried who answered that they would "almost always" or "most of the time" confide in someone, from 49 to 35 percent. Unfortunately, however, the questions were not exactly parallel. The 1991 question ("v246") asked about telling "someone (else) in your personal life"; the 2002 question ("SN13") asked simply about "someone (else)." Although a surface reading might suggest that the second version should have pushed respondents to answer *more* positively—it refers to a larger population of potential confidants—it may have been understood quite differently: the 1991 question

makes it clear that the respondent is being asked about what he or she says to intimates; the 2002 version may be understood as asking whether the respondent talks about such matters with anyone.

(2) One caution in such comparisons of Americans' relationships with their spouses is whether the population of Americans who were married changed over the decade. If people in troubled relationships were substantially likelier to avoid getting married or to get divorced in 2002 than in 1991, then that might produce an apparent improvement in the marriages of average married Americans. But the percentage of Americans age eighteen to fifty-four who were married changed little between 1992 and 2002. In 1992, 59 percent of Americans were married, while in 2002, 56 percent were (calculated from *Statistical Abstracts*). In the National Comorbidity Studies, however, it appears that 65 percent of the eighteen- to fifty-four-year-olds in the first survey were married, and about 55 percent in the second survey (Kessler et al. 2004, 85).

18.   Marginals from the Harris polls came from Roper Center, iPoll, USHARRIS.79PRIV.R03A, USHARRIS.90EQUI.RJ7A. Note that the first poll was done in person and the second over the telephone.

19.   These items come from the Gallup organization via http://institution.gallup.com/ (by subscription only). The specific items were: 1950—poll 460, item "qn4a"; 1989 (May)—Family Ties Survey, item "qn7"; 1990 (January, wave 2)—items "qn1" and "qn13f." The printed 1950 distribution is of numbers of *replies* (35 percent); re-norming to estimate the distribution of *persons* yields the 37 percent estimate.

20.   GSS items "numcntct" and "numprobs"; weight = "compwt," as in all analyses.

21.   GSS items "trtasian", "trtblack," "trthisp," "trtwhite." See DiPrete et al. (forthcoming) for analysis of these data.

22.   GSS item "talkedto." There is a statistically significant difference between the years, but it is not substantial: 59 percent of 2004's respondents versus 56 percent of 2002's respondents said that they talked at least once a month. The other questions in the series asked about helping "someone outside of your household with housework or shopping" (21 percent had not in the previous year); lending "quite a bit of money to another person" (53 percent had not in 2002, and 44 percent had not in 2004); and helping "somebody to find a job" (39 percent had not).

23.   Fischer (2009); McPherson et al. (2009).

24.   Swindle et al. (2000, table 2). See also Pescosolido et al. (2010) and Veroff, Douvan, and Kulka (1981, 481–83). Peter Marsden (personal communication, May 21, 2010) has suggested that this trend may reflect a drop in the stigmatization of mental illness.

25.   GSS items "famper1" through "famper5."

26.   For married respondents, the percentages reporting trouble were 4 and 3 percent for 1991 and 2004, respectively; for the unmarried, 2 percent in each

year reported trouble. Those who were likelier to report such problems were younger, had been married, and had babies in the home.

27. Overall, women, younger respondents, those with teenagers in the home, and, as one would expect, those separated or divorced at the time of the interview more often reported having broken up. Even with controls, the year effect for the never-married and formerly married remains statistically significant ($e^b = 2.1$ and 1.7, respectively).

28. U.S. Bureau of the Census, "Statistical Abstract Table 126: Marriages and Divorces: Number and Rate, by State," available at: http://www.census.gov/compendia/statab/2010/tables/10s0126.xls (accessed March 3, 2010).

29. Bumpass and Lu (2000, 33); Smock (2000).

30. In the total sample combining 1991 and 2004, the coefficient for year predicting trouble with a close friend, after controls, is not significant. Those reporting trouble tended to be younger, male, college graduates, and (an interaction effect) unmarried college graduates. (Put another way, unmarried college graduates were especially likely to report trouble.) Looking only at the (weighted) 7 percent who reported a breakup, the zero-order effect of year = 2004 is marginally significant ($p = .055$; $e^b = 2.4$), and the partial effect after controls is just significant ($p = .045$; $e^b = 2.6$).

31. With control variables in logit equations, the 2004 versus 1991 contrast in the total sample is statistically significant ($e^b = 1.6$), and the major predictors are age (complaints peaked around age forty), being female, less educated, or ever-married, having an eighteen- to twenty-four-year-old in the home, and, most especially, having a thirteen- to seventeen-year-old in the home. Dividing the sample by age of children, the year effect is not independently significant for those with a child under twenty-five in the home ($e^b = 1.4$), but is significant for those without ($e^b = 2.2$).

32. The largest year contrast was among respondents age forty-six to fifty-five. In 1991, 1 percent complained of serious trouble with a child; in 2004, 7 percent did. A rough estimate would be that the children in question were likely to be twenty-somethings.

33. The major exception would be the one-fourth reported by McPherson, Smith-Lovin, and Brashears (2006), which is anomalous and perhaps an error (Fischer 2009).

Chapter 6

1. For example, Lears (1983), Wuthnow (1994), and Stearns (1999).

2. Overviews of the literature conclude that there is a weak connection between "objective" measures of being alone (including living alone) and expressions of feeling lonely on various social psychological scales; see, for example, Peplau and Perlman (1982), Gierveld (1998), and Cacioppo and Patrick (2008). Examples of empirical studies include Alwin, Converse, and Martin (1985), Cornwell and Waite (2009a, 2009b [where they report a 0.25 correla-

tion but mix loneliness measures in with support measures]), Cutrona (1986), Dykstra, van Tilburg, and de Jong Gierveld (2005), Fischer and Phillips (1982), Jones and Moore (1987), Routasalo et al. (2006), Rubenstein and Shaver (1982), Schnittker (2007), and Victor et al. (2005). An ironic finding reported by John Cacioppo, James Fowler, and Nicholas Christakis (2009) is that feelings of loneliness spread *through* people's personal networks.

3. The zero-order correlations of the "socializing" items with the "loneliness" item are all under $r = .04$. A logit regression, with answering four days or more to the "loneliness" question as the dependent variable, shows significant effects for being unmarried, older, and uneducated. A combined scale ("socrel," "soccommun," "socfrend," and "socbar") is significantly associated with fewer lonely days ($p < .01$). Substantively, however, it remains a weak association.

4. Using the original data for the first and last polls in the series, I found that the increase in loneliness reports held for both married and unmarried respondents.

5. The WVS questions are: "For each of the following aspects, indicate how important it is in your life. Would you say it is: very important, rather important, not very important, or not important at all . . . family, friends, work." The source is the online analysis program of the WVS at http://www.world valuessurvey.org/.

6. Combining "great deal" and "good deal" yields an average of 77 percent reporting satisfaction and shows almost no fluctuation. In logit analyses of the probability of saying "very great deal," the zero-order effect of year is not significant; with controls, it is weakly positive, and given the n, significant ($e^b = 1.01$). Being married roughly quadrupled the chances of saying a "great deal" over the never-married, and more than doubled the chances over the ex-married. Women, whites, the educated, and those with babies were also likelier to say "great deal." An OLS regression using the entire range of the satisfaction scale yields similar results, with a negligible positive effect of year on satisfaction, beta = .025 ($p < .001$, n = 23,797).

7. For 1975 through 1977, 68 percent generally or definitely agreed; in 1984, 67 percent did (excluding members of one-person households, who were interviewed only in 1984).

8. I ran logit regressions both ways, with the dependent variable as (a) "wants much more time" versus other answers (overall, 44 percent wanted much more), and (b) "wants a bit more time" or "wants much more time" versus other answers (overall, 79 percent wanted more). For the first variant, the zero-order effects are that respondents in 1998 had about one and a half times the odds of saying "much more" than did respondents in 1989, and respondents in 2006 had about two and a half times the odds. After controls— "much more time" answers were especially likely to come from respondents who were working full-time, were less educated, were currently or had ever been married, and/or had babies—the residual effects were odds of 1.6 and 2.8. Adding number of hours worked in the previous week to the equation for those working did not improve prediction. The analyses for (b),

"wants a bit more time" or "wants much more time," yielded similar but "softer" results. Running OLS models with the full scale, from "wants much less" to "wants much more," as the dependent variable yielded similar results: zero-order betas of .09 and .19 for 1998 and 2006 and identical partial betas with several control variables.

9.   The overall percentage who volunteered that "it depends" also increased, from about 14 percent to 19 percent, which means that the percentage who said that it was a bad idea for older people to live with their grown children plummeted from 50 to 30 percent. The zero-order effect for year on the probability of saying it was a good idea is $e^b = 1.02$. Adding controls— respondents who lived in a three-generation household, who were younger, male, nonwhite, and never-married, and who had children at home were likelier to approve—leaves year at $e^b = 1.02$. (The multivariate analysis could be done only for 1975 to 2008 because the "generations in the household" measure is not available for 1972 to 1974.) Interaction terms with marital status and year are significant, given the large n, but add little to the pseudo-R-squared.

10.   For example, the category "entertaining friends and relatives" appears in the published results only between 1966 and 1978, with about 4 percent giving that answer. It is unlikely that fewer than 1 percent gave such answers in 1960 and after 1978. It is likely that the category "visit with friends or relatives" came to incorporate both the respondent going to their homes and having them come to the respondent's home. More critically, the category "be home with my family" does not appear in 1960.

11.   I simply fit quadratic equations through the points. Note that there is no point in 1960 for "home with family," so I left it out rather than assign it a zero.

12.   In Gallup's own published report on these data, the rise of the "family" answer in the 2000s is sharper than that shown here. I drew my numbers from the reports online at Gallup Brain (http://institution.gallup.com/). Carroll (2006) reports 32 percent as the percentage "staying home with family" for 2005, but the online record is 25 percent, which I use. The discrepancy arises, it appears, because Carroll included in the family category the answers "staying home" (6 percent) and "dinner at home" (1 percent), which, of course, are not the same thing, and their inclusion is inconsistent with the practice for earlier years.

13.   Time-budget data show a rise in hours watched from 1965 to 1975 and then slow growth or stagnation afterwards (Robinson and Martin 2009, 78–79; see also U.S. Bureau of the Census, *Statistical Abstract 2010*, "Table 1094: Media Usage and Consumer Spending", available at: http://www.census.gov/compendia/statab/2010/tables/10s1094.xls [accessed March 5, 2010]). The GSS variable, "tvhours" (in both raw and logged form), shows little change between 1975 and 2008.

14.   Calculated from Gallup "Lifestyle" polls, December 2002 and December 2005, via Gallup Brain (http://institution.gallup.com/).

15. The question was: "Are you satisfied with the number of friends you have, or would you like to have more?" The surveys were administered by Gallup, except in 1993, when it was conducted by Princeton Survey Research Associates. PSRA was established in 1989 by a group from Gallup, so we can assume continuity in procedures (iPoll: USGALLUP.90FRND.R02, USPSRA.93JUN1.R46, USGALLUP.01DC06.R43, USGALLUP.03DBR11.R21).

16. In 1986 the Gordon Black organization asked a national sample how "happy" they were with "the number of friends" they had: 70 percent said that they were "very happy," and 25 percent said that they were "somewhat happy" (Roper Center, iPoll, USGBUSA.869188.Q030). In 2009 Pew asked respondents how satisfied they were with "the number of friends" they had: 67 percent said that they were "very" satisfied, and 24 percent said that they were "somewhat" satisfied (iPoll: USPSRA.062909S.R02C). One could wonder whether "happy" and "satisfied" mean the same thing, but the results are strikingly similar and trendless.

17. Veroff, Douvan, and Kulka (1981), 117.

18. The dependent variable in a logit analysis is GSS item "peoplegn"—yes, the respondent had made "any effort" to search for friends versus "no effort." Pooling 2000 and 2002, people who reported having made any such effort (about 40 percent of the sample) tended to be younger, more educated, unmarried, and with no infants at home. Adding the natural log of the variable "numcntct" (answers to the question "Not counting people at work or family at home, about how many other friends or relatives do you keep in contact with at least once a year?") increases the pseudo-R-squared notably, and its coefficient is positive ($e^b = 1.3$; that is, people who reported having more ties also reported trying to make more friends). For 2002 alone, the variable "numprob" provides estimates of the number of people in whom respondents could confide. A logged version of that variable is also significantly positively associated, to the same degree, with the respondent having made any effort to meet new friends.

19. A logit analysis of rating the amount of satisfaction with friendships at "a very great deal" showed no effect of year after several controls. Such satisfaction was more common among women, whites, the educated, the never-married, those not keeping house, and those without young children at home. Interestingly, married respondents were likelier to say that they were highly satisfied, except that introducing the variable "satfam" ("satisfied a very great deal with family," dichotomized) reverses the effect of marriage. Apparently, individual tendencies to be upbeat about relationships (or just to be upbeat in answering surveys) suppressed a negative effect of being married on satisfaction with friends—which would be consistent with research suggesting that marriages strain at least preexisting friendships. (Using OLS on the full, seven-point "satisfaction with friends" scale tells the same story, except for this: introducing satisfaction with the family, "satfam," into the controls makes year marginally—but not substantively—significant, at beta = −.016, $p < .01$, n = 23,767.)

20. Unfortunately, not only is the Roper series unavailable from the Roper Center at the University of Connecticut, but this variable is not included in the Brady et al. (2000) data file. And surveys done after 1994 by Roper Starch are not publicly available.

21. In a more complex analysis, dividing the dependent variable at wants "much more" versus other answers shows statistically significant but small increases with year after controlling for covariates (e^b for 1998 = 1.2 and for 2006 = 1.3 versus 1989). Dividing it at wants "much more" or "a bit more" versus other answers shows a statistically significant but small independent effect of 2006 versus 1989: $e^b = 0.84$, $p < .05$ ($e^b = 0.77$, $p < .001$, without controls). Deeper analyses suggest that the respondents were divided between a majority who wanted more family *and* more friend time and a minority who wanted more time for work or household chores.

22. The 2006 interviews were face-to-face, and there are suggestions in the data that perhaps under those conditions respondents were pressed to be more explicit about trading off time among family, friends, jobs, and housework.

23. A popular introduction is Gosling (2008, ch. 2). The psychology journals are full of studies using the formulation. One overview is John, Naumann, and Soto (2008).

24. See, for example, "The Big Five Personality Test," available at: http://www.outofservice.com/bigfive/ (accessed November 12, 2010).

25. A search of databases finds essentially nothing since 1990 except for Twenge (2001), who cites a few fragmentary studies suggesting an increase in Americans' extroversion. Her own research entails meta-analyses of personality tests given mainly to college students; she concludes that there was a strong increase in extroversion. The 2001 paper is part of a series of such meta-analyses on various personality dimensions that have raised methodological concerns (Trzesniewski, Donnellan, and Robins 2008; Trzesniewski and Donnellan, forthcoming). I have bracketed her study in this discussion.

26. The correlations of the four-point scale constructed from the three items in figure 6.10 with GSS variables "numgiven" (in 1987, which is the only year both sets of questions were asked of the same respondents), "socfrend", "socrel," "friends," "numfrend," "frinum," "frivisit," and "famper5" range from −.08 (respondents who scored as more trusting reported *less* frequent visits with a best friend) to +.18 (respondents who scored as more trusting named more people in answer to the "important matters" question). The partial associations, controlling for key predictors and, where appropriate, year, range from about zero to +.14. The higher correlations are substantive, but not at the level we would expect if trusting as measured by this scale drove behavior with family and friends.

27. In 1987 (the only year the same respondents answered both types of questions) 56 percent of those scoring zero on the scale named three or more people to the "numgiven" question. Across the GSS years, 25 percent of the least trusting reported spending social evenings with friends ("socfrend") at least

several times a week, compared to 20 percent of those who were most trusting. See also note 26.

28. The discussion here draws from Fischer (2010, 192–93, and 324, notes 68, 69). Overviews of the topic include Smith (1997), Uslaner (2002), Putnam (2000, ch. 8), and Nannestad (2008). See also page 19.

On the rise and fall of trust, the iPoll database at the Roper Center provides the results for several NORC polls from 1948 to 1966 that used only the first part of the question, "Can people be trusted, yes or no?" (and one in 1960 that provided both options). A 1983 survey experiment by the GSS using both versions of the question shows that the standard version, which presents the alternative answer option of "you can't be too careful," produced a much lower percentage of respondents saying that most people can be trusted— by more than twenty percentage points. (Compare GSS items labeled "trust" and "trusty." GSS director Tom Smith [personal communication, February 4, 2010] reports that the GSS did not conduct a more thorough analysis of this survey experiment.) Using this experiment to apply a twenty-point downward adjustment to the NORC survey results from 1948 to 1966 suggests that trusting replies rose sharply after the war, peaked around 1963, and fell more or less steadily for nearly four decades.

29. I examined results for the central question—can most people be trusted?— from the American National Election Survey, the World Values Survey, Pew surveys done by Princeton Survey Research Associates, and a handful of polls by Gallup. Although considerably noisier, together they confirm the general downward trend shown in figure 6.10.

30. Again, see Fischer (2010, 192–93, and notes) and Nannestad (2008) for recent surveys of that literature.

31. In support of this claim, I would point to a couple of items of evidence. One is the low correlation in the GSS data between the trust scale and items measuring personal ties (see note 26). These weak associations contrast with higher correlations between the same trust scale and items measuring *public* participation (–.25 with "locvote," how often they vote in local elections; –.20 with whether they voted in the last presidential election [respondents age twenty-one and up only]; –.18 with interest in politics ["intpol"]; and –.18 with organizational memberships ["memnum"]). Another piece of evidence is provided by studies that show trust to be greatly affected by levels of local ethnic and class diversity. Costa and Kahn (2003a, 39, note 14), for example, report that increasing community heterogeneity explains 32 percent of the longitudinal trend in the GSS most people can be trusted item (see also Putnam 2007). Readers will recognize a distinction here similar to Robert Putnam's (2000) between "bonding" and "bridging" ties.

32. One data series—Roper—contradicts this conclusion, but the other data are consistent.

Chapter 7

1.   Wang and Wellman (2010).

2. Survey response rates declined over the 1970 to 2010 period. One possibility is that survey researchers increasingly missed the socially isolated and corrected for that by demographic weighting. Yet we can also argue that it was the socially active—those who were too often out of the home, more likely to use a cell phone than a landline, or too busy to answer pollsters—who were increasingly missed. One reassurance comes from a close study of nonresponse in the two National Comorbidity Studies. The response rate dropped from 80 to 71 percent between 1990 to 1992 and 2001 to 2003. However, the undercount of the psychologically disordered (who would more often tend to be the socially isolated) actually shrank (Kessler et al. 2004), suggesting a tilt, if any, toward the later surveys including more of the less connected. The concern about coverage should also lead us to place more emphasis on the GSS than the commercial surveys because the GSS response rates, although they also slumped, remained much higher.

3. Deresiewicz (2009); Nie quoted in John Markoff, "A Newer, Lonelier Crowd Emerges in Internet," *New York Times*, February 16, 2000.

4. Quoted in Fishkoff and Palevsky (2010, 24).

5. Lisa Guernsey, "Cyberspace Isn't So Lonely After All," *New York Times*, July 26, 2001.

6. These conclusions are my gloss of the literature (some of which is listed here), amended by advice from Barry Wellman, Helen Hua Wang, and Jeffrey Boase—provided online, of course (personal communications, March 9–15, 2010)—although they are not blameworthy for the final formulations. The literature on the topic is growing exponentially. Overviews include, in chronological order: DiMaggio et al. (2001); Haythornwaite and Wellman (2002); Bargh and McKenna (2004); Wellman (2004); Shklovski, Kraut, and Rainie (2006); and Boase and Wellman (2006). Some important and/or recent studies, in alphabetical order, include: Boase (2008); Boneva and Kraut (2002); Collins and Wellman (2010); Gennaro and Dutton (2007); Hampton and Wellman (2001, 2003); Hampton, Sessions, and Her (2009); Howard (2004); Howard, Rainie, and Jones (2002); Katz, Rice, and Aspden (2001); Kennedy et al. (2008); Lebo (2009); Nie, Hillygus, and Erbring (2002; compare Witte 2004, xvi); Quell et al. (2007); Rainie and Wellmann (2011); and Wang and Wellman (2010).

7. In 2000, 2002, and 2004, the GSS asked respondents to estimate the number of people with whom they were in contact at least once a year ("numcntct") and then asked how many of them they contacted in person, in meetings, or by email, letter, or phone. Reporting more persons contacted via telephone was associated—holding constant the total number of people with whom respondents said they were in contact so as to hold constant individual sociability—with reporting *more* people seen in person. Reporting more frequent email "partners" was not associated with more or less frequent in-person associates. That is, in the GSS data new media did not substitute for or undermine face-to-face contact.

8. Pescosolido et al. (2010)

9. See, in particular, Bianchi, Robinson, and Milkie (2006); Hofferth and Sandberg (2001); Ramey and Ramey (2010).

10. Costa and Kahn (2003a) credit women's employment for many of the changes in social activities that they examine. Some they also attribute to increasing income inequality and greater cultural diversity.

11. We might then expect women's social ties to have changed more than men's. I examined about a dozen of the GSS measures used in earlier chapters to see if the trends differed by gender. In short: not really. This may be evidence against the "women going to work" argument; alternatively, it is possible that changes in women's lives ramify to affect men's lives as well, or that the absence of any gender difference in these trends demonstrates the resilience of social ties (discussed later).

12. See Fischer (2010, especially chs. 4 and 6).

13. Although it has been argued that capitalism led to sentimentality; see, for example, Haskell (1985).

14. See discussion in Fischer (2010, ch. 4). On friendship in particular, see, for example, Silver (1990, 1997), Rotundo (1989), and Oliker (1998).

15. See, for example, Lareau (2002) and Stearns (2003).

16. See Fischer et al. (1977, 200–201):

> Individuals probably try to maintain networks with certain characteristics suited to each one's preferences. . . . [They] can anticipate the effects of certain changes and act accordingly to protect their networks. . . . And once some effect has occurred, they can adjust so as to restore the network structure (for example, letting some prior friendships lapse after having made some new friends). To the extent to which people can anticipate, adjust, decide, and act in these protective ways, their networks are resilient to outside forces and will "bounce back" to their original shapes. . . .
>
> For the empirical study of networks, these anticipations and adjustments mean that, although it may be in principle true that structural factors have great effects on networks . . . those effects would not be seen in a cross-sectional study of the general population, because, at any given moment, most people are maintaining networks within the narrow, common range.

17. Fischer (1992).

18. See, for example, Ferraro (1984); Morgan and March (1992); van Baarsen et al. (2001–2002); Utz et al. (2002); D'Epinay, Cavalli, and Spini (2003); Dykstra, van Tilburg, and de Jong Gierveld (2005); Li (2007).

19. See, for example, Consumer Reports, "Trim Your Cell-Phone Bill" (April 2009), available at: http://www.consumerreports.org/cro/money/shopping/ways-to-save-on/cell-phone-bills/overview/cell-phone-bills.htm (accessed July 23, 2010).

References

Agular, Mark, and Erik Hurst. 2007. "Measuring Trends in Leisure: The Allocation of Time over Five Decades." *Quarterly Journal of Economics* 122(3): 969–1006.

Alesina, Alberto, and Eliana La Ferrara. 2002. "Who Trusts Others?" *Journal of Public Economics* 85(2): 207–34.

Alwin, Duane F., Philip E. Converse, and Steven S. Martin. 1985. "Living Arrangements and Social Integration." *Journal of Marriage and the Family* 47(2): 319–34.

Amato, Paul R., Alan Booth, David R. Johnson, and Stacy J. Rogers. 2007. *Alone Together: How Marriage in America Is Changing.* Cambridge, Mass.: Harvard University Press.

Antonucci, Toni C., and Hiroko Akiyama. 1987. "Social Networks in Adult Life and a Preliminary Examination of the Convoy Model." *Journal of Gerontology* 42(5): 519–27.

Antonucci, Toni C., Hiroko Akiyama, and Jennifer E. Lansford. 1998. "Negative Effects of Close Social Relations." *Family Relations* 47(4): 379–84.

Antonucci, Toni C., Hiroko Akiyama, and Keiko Takahashi. 2004. "Attachment and Close Relationships Across the Life Span." *Attachment and Human Development* 6(4): 353–70.

Aquilino, William S. 1994. "Interview Mode Effects in Surveys of Drug and Alcohol Use: A Field Experiment." *Public Opinion Quarterly* 58(2): 210–40.

Arling, Greg. 1987. "Strain, Social Support, and Distress in Old Age." *Journal of Gerontology* 42(1): 107–13.

Arnett, Jeffrey Jensen. 1998. "Learning to Stand Alone: The Contemporary American Transition to Adulthood in Cultural and Historical Context." *Human Development* 41(5–6): 295–315.

———. 2004. *Emerging Adulthood: The Winding Road from the Late Teens Through the Twenties.* New York: Oxford University Press.

Arria, Amelia M., Kevin E. O'Grady, Kimberly M. Caldeira, Kathryn B. Vincent, Holly C. Wilcox, and Eric D. Wish. 2009. "Suicide Ideation Among College Students: A Multivariate Analysis." *Archives of Suicide Research* 13(3): 230–46.

Bahr, Howard M., Colter Mitchell, Xiaomin Li, Alison Walker, and Kristen Sucher. 2004. "Trends in Family Space/Time, Conflict, and Solidarity: Middletown, 1924–1999." *City and Community* 3(September): 263–91.

Bailey, Stefanie, and Peter V. Marsden. 1999. "Interpretation and Interview Context: Examining the General Social Survey Name Generator Using Cognitive Methods." *Social Networks* 21(3): 287–309.

Bargh, John H., and Katelyn Y. A. McKenna. 2004. "The Internet and Social Life." *Annual Review of Psychology* 55: 573–90.

Bearman, Peter S., James Moody, and Katherine Stovel. 2004. "Chains of Affection: The Structure of Adolescent Romantic and Sexual Networks." *American Journal of Sociology* 110(1): 44–91.

Bearman, Peter S., and Paolo Parigi. 2004. "Cloning Headless Frogs and Other Important Matters: Conversation Topics and Network Structure." *Social Forces* 83(December): 535–57.

Bell, David C., Benedetta Belli-McQueen, and Ali Haider. 2007. "Partner Naming and Forgetting: Recall of Network Members." *Social Networks* 29(May): 279–99.

Bellah, Robert N., Richard Madsen, William M. Sullivan, Ann Swidler, and Steven M. Tipton. 1985. *Habits of the Heart: Individualism and Commitment in American Life.* Berkeley: University of California Press.

Bernard, H. Russell, Eugene C. Johansen, Peter D. Killworth, Christopher McCarty, Gene A. Shelley, and Scott Robinson. 1990. "Comparing Four Different Methods for Measuring Personal Social Networks." *Social Networks* 12(3): 179–215.

Bianchi, Suzanne. 2007. "Changes in Time Allocation of American Parents, 1965 to the Present." Life Course Center "Miniconference." University of Minnesota, Minneapolis (October).

Bianchi, Suzanne, John P. Robinson, and Melissa A. Milkie. 2006. *Changing Rhythms of American Family Life.* New York: Russell Sage Foundation.

Bishop, George F., and Bonnie S. Fisher. 1995. " 'Secret Ballots' and Self-Reports in an Exit-Poll Experiment." *Public Opinion Quarterly* 59(4): 568–88.

Blau, Melinda, and Karen L. Fingerman. 2009. *Consequential Strangers: The Power of People Who Don't Seem to Matter . . . But Really Do.* New York: Norton.

Boase, Jeffrey. 2008. "Personal Networks and the Personal Communication System." *Information, Communication, and Society* 11(4): 490–508.

Boase, Jeffrey, and Barry Wellman. 2006. "Personal Relationships: On and Off the Internet." In *The Cambridge Handbook of Personal Relationships*, edited by Anita L. Vangelisti and Dan Perlman. New York: Cambridge University Press.

Boissevain, Jeremy. 1974. *Friends of Friends: Networks, Manipulators, and Coalitions.* New York: St. Martin's Press.

Boneva, Bonka, and Robert Kraut. 2002. "E-mail, Gender, and Personal Relationships." In *The Internet in Everyday Life*, edited by Barry Wellman and Caroline Haythornwaite. Malden, Mass.: Blackwell.

Borgatti, Stephen P., and Pacey C. Foster. 2003. "The Network Paradigm in Organizational Research: A Review and Typology." *Journal of Management* 29(6): 991–1013.

Brady, Henry E., Robert D. Putnam, Andrea L. Campbell, Laurel Elms, Steven Yonish, and Dorie Apollonio. 2000. *Roper Social and Political Trends Data, 1973–1994* (computer file). Individual surveys conducted by the Roper Organization and Roper Starch Worldwide (producers), 1973–1994. Storrs, Conn.: University of Connecticut, Roper Center for Public Opinion Research (distributor).

Brewer, Devon D. 2000. "Forgetting in the Recall-Based Elicitation of Personal and Social Networks." *Social Networks* 22(1): 29–44.

Bumpass, Larry, and Hsien-Hen Lu. 2000. "Trends in Cohabitation and Implications for Children's Family Contexts in the United States." *Population Studies* 54(1): 29–41.

Burt, Ronald S. 1984. "Network Items and the General Social Survey." *Social Networks* 6(4): 293–339.

Cacioppo, John T., James H. Fowler, and Nicholas A. Christakis. 2009. "Alone in the Crowd: The Structure and Spread of Loneliness in a Large Social Network." *Journal of Personality and Social Psychology* 97(6): 977–91.

Cacioppo, John T., and William Patrick. 2008. *Loneliness: Human Nature and the Need for Social Connection.* New York: Norton.

Carolina Population Center. 2009. "Add Health." Available at: http://cpc.unc.edu/projects/addhealth (accessed September 17, 2010).

Carroll, Joseph. 2006. "Family Time Eclipses TV as Favorite Way to Spend an Evening." Gallup News Service, March 10, available at: http://www.gallup.com/poll/21856/Family-Time-Eclipses-Favorite-Way-Spend-Evening.aspx (accessed September 17, 2010).

Christakis, Nicholas A., and James H. Fowler. 2009. *Connected: The Surprising Power of Our Social Networks and How They Shape Our Lives.* New York: Little, Brown.

Clark, Shelley, and Catherine Kenney. 2010. "Is the United States Experiencing a 'Matrilineal Tilt?' " *Social Forces* 88(June): 1753–76.

Cohany, Sharon R., and Emy Sok. 2007. "Trends in Labor Force Participation of Married Mothers of Infants." *Monthly Labor Review* 130(2): 9–16.

Cohen, Sheldon, and Denise Janicki-Deverts. 2009. "Can We Improve Our Physical Health by Altering Our Social Networks?" *Perspectives on Psychological Science* 4(4): 375–78.

Cohen-Cole, Ethan, and Jason M. Fletcher. 2008. "Detecting Implausible Social Network Effects in Acne, Height, and Headaches: Longitudinal Analysis." *British Medical Journal* (online first) (December 4): 337,a2533. Available at: doi:10.1136/bmj.a2533.

Coleman, James S. 1958–1959. "Relational Analysis: The Study of Social Organizations with Survey Methods." *Human Organization* 17(4): 28–36.

Coleman, James Samuel, Elihu Katz, and Herbert Menzel. 1966. *Medical Innovation: A Diffusion Study.* Indianapolis: Bobbs-Merrill.

Collins, Jessica L., and Barry Wellman. 2010. "Small Town in the Internet Society: Chapleau Is No Longer an Island." *American Behavioral Scientist* 53(9): 1344–66.

Converse, Jean M., and Stanley Presser. 1986. *Survey Questions: Handcrafting the Standardized Questionnaire.* Beverly Hills, Calif.: Sage Publications.

Cornwell, Erin York, and Linda J. Waite. 2009a. "Social Disconnectedness, Perceived Isolation, and Health Among Older Adults." *Journal of Health and Social Behavior* 50(1): 31–48.

———. 2009b. "Measuring Social Isolation Among Older Adults Using Multiple Indicators from the NSHAP study." *Journals of Gerontology Series B: Social Sciences* 64B(suppl1): 38–46.

Costa, Dora L., and Matthew E. Kahn. 2003a. "Understanding the American Decline in Social Capital, 1952–1998." *Kyklos* 56(1): 17–46.

———. 2003b. "Civic Engagement and Community Heterogeneity." *Perspectives on Politics* 1(March): 103–11.

Critchfield, Tim, Tyler Davis, Lee Davison, Heather Gratton, George Hanc, and Katherine Samolyk. 2005. "Community Banks: Their Recent Past, Current Performance, and Future Prospects." *FDIC Banking Review* (January). Available at: http://www.fdic.gov/bank/analytical/banking/2005jan/article1.html (accessed December 9, 2009).

Curtin, Richard, Stanley Presser, and Eleanor Singer. 2005. "Changes in Telephone Survey Nonresponse over the Past Quarter-Century." *Public Opinion Quarterly* 69(1): 87–98.

Cutrona, Carolyn E. 1986. "Objective Determinants of Perceived Social Support." *Journal of Personality and Social Psychology* 50(2): 349–55.

D'Epinay, Christian J. Lalive, Stefano Cavalli, and Dario Spini. 2003. "The Death of a Loved One: Impact on Health and Relationships in Very Old Age." *Omega* 47(3): 265–84.

Deresiewicz, William. 2009. "Faux Friendship." *Chronicle of Higher Education* (December 6). Available at: http://chronicle.com/article/Faux-Friendship/49308/ (accessed February 11, 2010).

DiMaggio, Paul, Eszter Hargittai, W. Russell Neuman, and John P. Robinson. 2001. "Social Implications of the Internet." *Annual Review of Sociology* 27: 307–36.

DiPrete, Thomas A., Tyler McCormick, Andrew Gelman, Julien Teitler, and Tian Zheng. Forthcoming. "Segregation in Social Networks Based on Acquaintanceship and Trust." *American Journal of Sociology.*

Dykstra, Pearl A., Theo G. van Tilburg, and Jenny de Jong Gierveld. 2005. "Change in Older Adult Loneliness: Results from a Seven-Year Longitudinal Study." *Research on Aging* 27(6): 725–47.

Erickson, Bonnie. 2003. "Social Networks: The Value of Variety." *Contexts* 2(1): 25–31.

Ertel, Karen A., M. Maria Glymour, and Lisa F. Berkman. 2009. "Social Networks and Health: A Life Course Perspective Integrating Observational and Experimental Evidence." *Journal of Social and Personal Relationships* 26(1): 73–92.

Falci, Christina, and Clea McNeely. 2009. "Too Many Friends: Social Integration, Network Cohesion, and Adolescent Depressive Symptoms." *Social Forces* 87(4): 2031–61.

Feld, Scott L. 1981. "The Focused Organization of Social Ties." *American Journal of Sociology* 86(5): 1015–35.

Ferraro, Kenneth F. 1984. "Widowhood and Social Participation in Later Life: Isolation or Compensation?" *Research on Aging* 6(4): 451–68.

Fischer, Claude S. 1973. Review essay in "Review Symposium," on Packard, *A Nation of Strangers. American Journal of Sociology* 79(July): 168–73.

———. 1981. "The Public and Private Worlds of City Life." *American Sociological Review* 46(3): 306–16.

———. 1982a. *To Dwell Among Friends: Personal Networks in Town and City.* Chicago: University of Chicago Press.

———. 1982b. "What Do We Mean by 'Friend'?" *Social Networks* 3(4): 287–306.

———. 1983. "The Friendship Cure-All." *Psychology Today* 17(1): 74, 78.

———. 1984. *The Urban Experience.* 2d ed. New York: Harcourt.

———. 1992. *America Calling: A Social History of the Telephone to 1940*. Berkeley: University of California Press.

———. 2000. "Just How Is It That Americans Are Individualistic?" Paper presented to the American Sociological Association, Washington (August). Available at: http://sociology.berkeley.edu/profiles/fischer/pubs.php (accessed November 12, 2010).

———. 2005. "Bowling Alone: What's the Score?" (review essay). *Social Networks* 27(May): 155–67.

———. 2009. "The 2004 GSS Finding of Shrunken Social Networks: An Artifact?" *American Sociological Review* 74(4): 657–69.

———. 2010. *Made in America: A Social History of American Culture and Character*. Chicago: University of Chicago Press.

Fischer, Claude S., and Michael Hout. 2006. *Century of Difference: How America Changed in the Last One Hundred Years*. New York: Russell Sage Foundation.

Fischer, Claude S., Robert Max Jackson, Charlotte Stueve, Kathleen Gerson, and Lynne McCallister Jones, with Mark Baldassare. 1977. *Networks and Places: Social Relations in the Urban Setting*. New York: Free Press.

Fischer, Claude S., and Susan Phillips. 1982. "Who Is Alone: Social Characteristics of People with Small Networks." In *Loneliness: A Sourcebook of Current Research*, edited by Letitia Anne Peplau and Daniel Perlman. New York: Wiley.

Fishkoff, Sue, and Stacey Palevsky. 2010. "cu @ temple." *J* (January 8): 24–25. Available at JWeekly.com, http://www.jweekly.com/article/full/40966/cu-temple-social-media-transforming-the-way-synagogues-members-connect/ (accessed November 12, 2010).

Freeman, Linton C. 2004. *The Development of Social Network Analysis: A Study in the Sociology of Science*. Vancouver, B.C.: Empirical Press.

Friedman, Lawrence M. 1990. *The Republic of Choice: Law, Authority, and Culture*. Cambridge, Mass.: Harvard University Press.

Furstenberg, Frank F., Jr., Sheela Kennedy, Vonnie C. McLoyd, Rubén G. Rumbaut, and Richard A. Settersten. 2004. "Growing Up Is Harder to Do." *Contexts* 3(July): 33–41.

Gans, Daphna, and Merril Silverstein. 2006. "Norms of Filial Responsibility for Aging Parents Across Time and Generations." *Journal of Marriage and Family* 68(4): 961–76.

Gennaro, Corinna di, and William H. Dutton. 2007. "Reconfiguring Friendships: Social Relationships and the Internet." *Information, Communication, and Society* 10(5): 591–618.

Gergen, Kenneth J. 2000. "The Self in the Age of Information." *Washington Quarterly* 23(1): 201–14.

Giddens, Anthony. 1991. *Modernity and Self-Identity: Self and Society in the Late Modern Age*. Stanford, Calif.: Stanford University Press.

Gierveld, Jenny de Jong. 1998. "A Review of Loneliness: Concept and Definitions, Determinants and Consequences." *Reviews in Clinical Gerontology* 8(1): 78–80.

Gillis, John. 1996. "Making Time for Family: The Invention of Family Time(s) and the Reinvention of Family History." *Journal of Family History* 21(January): 4–21.

Gosling, Sam. 2008. *Snoop: What Your Stuff Says About You*. New York: Basic Books.

Granovetter, Mark. 1973. "The Strength of Weak Ties." *American Journal of Sociology* 78(May): 1360–80.

————. 1995. *Getting a Job: A Study of Contacts and Careers.* 2d ed. Cambridge, Mass.: Harvard University Press. (Orig. pub. in 1974.)

Guest, Avery M., and Susan K. Wierzbicki. 1999. "Social Ties at the Neighborhood Level: Two Decades of GSS Evidence." *Urban Affairs Review* 35(September): 92–111.

Hampton, Keith N., Lauren F. Sessions, and Eun Ja Her. 2009. "Americans' Core Networks: Social Isolation and the Use of the Internet and Cell Phones." Paper presented to meetings of the American Sociological Association, San Francisco (August).

Hampton, Keith, and Barry Wellman. 2001. "Long-Distance Community in the Network Society: Contact and Support Beyond Netville." *American Behavioral Scientist* 45(3): 476–95.

————. 2003. "Neighboring in Netville: How the Internet Supports Community and Social Capital in a Wired Suburb." *City and Community* 2(4): 277–311.

Haskell, Thomas L. 1985. "Capitalism and the Origins of the Humanitarian Sensibility: Part 1." *American Historical Review* 90(April): 339–61.

Haythornwaite, Caroline, and Barry Wellman. 2002. "The Internet in Everyday Life." In *The Internet in Everyday Life,* edited by Barry Wellman and Caroline Haythornwaite. Malden, Mass.: Blackwell.

Hofferth, Sandra L., and John F. Sandberg. 2001. "Changes in American Children's Time, 1981–1997." *Advances in Life Course Research* 6: 193–229.

Holt-Lunstad, Julianne, Timothy B. Smith, and J. Bradley Layton. 2010. "Social Relationships and Mortality Risk: A Meta-Analytic Review." *PLoS Med* 7(7). Available at: http://www.plosmedicine.org/article/info:doi/10.1371/journal.pmed.1000316 (accessed November 12, 2010).

Howard, Philip N. 2004. "Embedded Media, Who We Know, What We Know, and Society Online." In *Society Online: The Internet in Context,* edited by Philip N. Howard and Steve Jones. Thousand Oaks, Calif.: Sage Publications.

Howard, Philip E. N., Lee Rainie, and Steve Jones. 2002. "Days and Nights on the Internet." In *The Internet in Everyday Life,* edited by Barry Wellman and Caroline Haythornwaite. Malden, Mass.: Blackwell.

Ikkink, Karen Klein, Theo van Tilburg, and Kees C. P. M. Knipscheer. 1999. "Perceived Instrumental Support Exchanges in Relationships Between Elderly Parents and Their Adult Children: Normative and Structural Explanations." *Journal of Marriage and the Family* 61(4): 831–44.

Jackman, Mary R., and Robert W. Jackman. 1983. *Class Awareness in the United States.* Berkeley: University of California Press.

John, Oliver P., Laura P. Naumann, and Christopher J. Soto. 2008. "Paradigm Shift to the Integrative Big-Five Trait Taxonomy: History, Measurement, and Conceptual Issues." In *Handbook of Personality: Theory and Research,* 3d ed., edited by Oliver P. John, Richard W. Robins, and Lawrence A. Pervin. New York: Guilford Press.

Jones, Kenneth D., and Tim Critchfield. 2006. "Consolidation in the U.S. Banking Industry: Is the 'Long, Strange Trip' About to End?" *FDIC Banking Review* (January). Available at: http://www.fdic.gov/bank/analytical/banking/2006jan/article2/index.html (accessed December 9, 2009).

Jones, Warren H., and Teri L. Moore. 1987. "Loneliness and Social Support." *Journal of Social Behavior and Personality* 2(2): 145–56.

Kadushin, Charles. 2004. "Too Much Investment in Social Capital." *Social Networks* 26(1): 75–90.

Katz, Elihu. 1957. "The Two-Step Flow of Communication: An Up-to-Date Report on an Hypothesis." *Public Opinion Quarterly* 21(1): 61–78.

Katz, Elihu, and Paul F. Lazarsfeld. 1955. *Personal Influence: The Part Played by People in the Flow of Mass Communications.* Glencoe, Ill.: Free Press.

Katz, James E., Ronald E. Rice, and Philip Aspden. 2001. "The Internet, 1995–2000: Access, Civic Involvement, and Social Interaction." *American Behavioral Scientist* 45(3): 405–19.

Keeter, Scott, Courtney Kennedy, April Clark, Trevor Tompson, and Mike Mokrzycki. 2007. "What's Missing from National Landline RDD Surveys? The Impact of the Growing Cell-Only Population." *Public Opinion Quarterly* 71(5): 772–92.

Kennedy, Tracy L. M., Aaron Smith, Amy Tracy Wells, and Barry Wellman. 2008. "Networked Families." Washington, D.C.: Pew Internet and American Life Project.

Kessler, Ronald C. 1992. "Perceived Support and Adjustment to Stress: Methodological Considerations." In *The Meaning and Measurement of Social Support,* edited by Hans O. F. Veiel and Urs Baumann. New York: Hemisphere.

Kessler, Ronald C., Patricia Berglund, Wai T. Chiu, Olga Demler, Steven Heeringa, Eva Hiripi, Robert Jin, Beth-Ellen P. Pennell, Ellen E. Walters, Alan Zaslavsky, and Hui Zheng. 2004. "The U.S. National Comorbidity Survey Replication (NCS-R): Design and Field Procedures." *International Journal of Methods in Psychiatric Research* 13(2): 69–92.

Keum, Heejo, Narayan Devanathan, Sameer Deshpande, Michelle R. Nelson, and Dhavan V. Shah. 2004. "The Citizen-Consumer: Media Effects at the Intersection of Consumer and Civic Culture." *Political Communication* 21(3): 369–91.

Kiefer, Heather Mason. 2004. "Empty Seats: Fewer Families Eat Together." Gallup News Service, January 20. Available at: http://www.gallup.com/poll/10336/Empty-Seats-Fewer-Families-Eat-Together.aspx (accessed November 12, 2010).

Killworth, Peter, Eugene Johnson, H. Russell Bernard, Gene Ann Shelley, and Christopher McCarthy. 1990. "Estimating the Size of Personal Networks." *Social Networks* 12(4): 289–312.

Klofstad, Casey A., Scott D. McClurg, and Meredith Rolfe. 2009. "Measurement of Political Discussion Networks: A Comparison of Two 'Name Generator' Procedures." *Public Opinion Quarterly* 73(3): 462–83.

Krause, Neal, and Elaine Borawski-Clark. 1994. "Clarifying the Functions of Social Support in Later Life." *Research on Aging* 16(3): 251–79.

Krysan, Maria. 1998. "Privacy and the Expression of White Racial Attitudes: A Comparison Across Three Contexts." *Public Opinion Quarterly* 62(4): 506–44.

Lareau, Annette. 2002. "Invisible Inequality: Social Class and Childrearing in Black Families and White Families." *American Sociological Review* 67(5): 747–76.

Laumann, Edward O. 1966. *Prestige and Association in an Urban Community: An Analysis of an Urban Stratification System.* Indianapolis: Bobbs-Merrill.

———. 1973. *Bonds of Pluralism: The Form and Substance of Urban Social Networks.* New York: Wiley.

Lears, T. J. Jackson. 1983. "From Salvation to Self-Realization: Advertising and the Therapeutic Roots of the Consumer Culture, 1880–1930." In *The Culture of Consumption*, by Richard Wightman Fox and T. J. Jackson Lears. New York: Pantheon.

Lebo, Harlan. 2009. "The 2009 Digital Future Report: Surveying the Digital Future, Year Eight: Fifteen Years of Internet Use." Los Angeles: University of Southern California, Annenberg School Center for the Digital Future.

Leffler, Ann, Richard S. Krannich, and Dair L. Gillespie. 1986. "Contact, Support, and Friction: Three Faces of Networks in Community Life." *Sociological Perspectives* 29(3): 337–55.

Leib, Ethan J. 2007. "Friendship and the Law." *UCLA Law Review* 54: 631–707.

Li, Yunging. 2007. "Recovering from Spousal Bereavement in Later Life: Does Volunteer Participation Play a Role?" *Journals of Gerontology, Series B: Psychological Sciences and Social Sciences* 62B(4): S257–66.

Lin, Nan. 1999. "Social Networks and Status Attainment." *Annual Review of Sociology* 25: 467–87.

Lundberg, George A., and Mary Steele. 1938. "Social Attraction-Patterns in a Village." *Sociometry* 1(3–4): 375–419.

Marin, Alexandra. 2004. "Are Respondents More Likely to List Alters with Certain Characteristics? Implications for Name Generator Data." *Social Networks* 26(4): 289–307.

Marin, Alexandra, and Keith N. Hampton. 2007. "Simplifying the Personal Network Name Generator." *Field Methods* 19(2): 163–93.

Marin, Alexandra, and Barry Wellman. 2010. "Social Network Analysis: An Introduction." In *Handbook of Social Network Analysis*, edited by Peter Carrington and John Scott. London: Sage Publications.

Marsden, Peter V. 1987. "Core Discussion Networks of Americans." *American Sociological Review* 52(February): 122–31.

———. 1990. "Network Data and Measurement." *Annual Review of Sociology* 16: 435–63.

———. 2003. "Interviewer Effects in Measuring Network Size Using a Single Name Generator." *Social Networks* 25(1): 1–16.

———. 2005. "Recent Developments in Network Measurement." In *Models and Methods in Social Network Analysis*, edited by Peter J. Carrington, John Scott, and Stanley Wasserman. New York: Cambridge University Press.

———. 2010. "Survey Methods for Network Data." In *Sage Handbook of Social Network Analysis*, edited by John Scott and Peter Carrington. London: Sage Publications.

Marsden, Peter V., and Karen E. Campbell. 1984. "Measuring Tie Strength." *Social Forces* 63(2): 482–501.

Marsden, Peter V. and Sameer B. Srivastava. 2011. "Trends in Informal Social Participation, 1974–2008." In *Social Trends in the United States, 1972–2000s: Evidence from the General Social Survey*, edited by Peter V. Marsden. Princeton, N.J.: Princeton University Press.

McCallister, Lynne, and Claude S. Fischer. 1978. "A Procedure for Surveying Personal Networks." *Sociological Methods and Research* 7(November): 131–48.

McCarty, Christopher, H. Russell Bernard, Peter D. Killworth, Gene A. Shelley, and Eugene C. Johnsen. 1997. "Eliciting Representative Samples of Personal Networks." *Social Networks* 19(4): 303–23.

McCarty, Christopher, Peter D. Killworth, H. Russell Bernard, Eugene C. Johnsen, and Gene A. Shelley. 2001. "Comparing Two Methods for Estimating Network Size." *Human Organization* 60(1): 28–39.

McGarry, Kathleen, and Robert F. Schoeni. 1997. "Transfer Behavior Within the Family: Results from the Asset and Health Dynamics Study." *Journals of Gerontology Series B: Psychological Sciences and Social Sciences* 52B(special issue): 82–92.

McPherson, Miller, Lynn Smith-Lovin, and Matthew E. Brashears. 2006. "Social Isolation in America: Changes in Core Discussion Networks over Two Decades." *American Sociological Review* 71(3): 353–75.

———. 2008. "Erratum: Social Isolation in America: Changes in Core Discussion Networks over Two Decades." *American Sociological Review* 73(6): 1022.

———. 2009. "Models and Marginals: Using Survey Evidence to Study Social Networks." *American Sociological Review* 74(4): 670–81.

Mollenhorst, Gerald. 2009. *Networks in Contexts: How Meeting Opportunities Affect Personal Relationships*. Utrecht, Netherlands: Utrecht University, Interuniversity Center for Social Science Theory and Methodology.

Morgan, David L., and Stephan J. March. 1992. "The Impact of Life Events on Networks of Personal Relationships: A Comparison of Widowhood and Caring for a Spouse with Alzheimer's Disease." *Journal of Social and Personal Relationships* 9(4): 563–84.

Morgan, David L., Margaret B. Neal, and Paula Carder. 1997. "The Stability of Core and Peripheral Networks over Time." *Social Networks* 19(1): 9–25.

Nannestad, Peter. 2008. "What Have We Learned About Generalized Trust—Anything?" *Annual Review of Political Science* 11: 413–36.

Nie, Norman H., D. Sunshine Hillygus, and Lutz Erbring. 2002. "Internet Use, Interpersonal Relations, and Sociability: A Time Diary Study." In *The Internet in Everyday Life*, edited by Barry Wellman and Caroline Haythornthwaite. Malden, Mass.: Blackwell.

Noll, A. Michael. 1994. "Comment: A Study of Long-Distance Rates." *Telecommunications Policy* 18(5): 355–62.

Norlev, Jeanette, Michael Davidsen, Vanita Sundaram, and Mette Kjoller. 2005. "Indicators Associated with Suicidal Ideation and Suicide Attempts Among Sixteen- to Thirty-five-Year-Old Danes: A National Representative Population Study." *Suicide and Life-Threatening Behavior* 35(3): 291–308.

NPD Group. 1999. "Americans Spending More Time on Themselves, Says NPD Study." Port Washington, N.Y.: NPD Group.

O'Brien, David J., and Valeri V. Patsiorkovsky. 2006. *Measuring Social and Economic Change in Rural Russia: Surveys from 1991 to 2003*. Latham, Md.: Lexington Books.

O'Brien, David J., Stephen K. Wegren, and Valeri V. Patsiorkovsky. 2005. "Marketization and Community in Post-Soviet Russian Villages." *Rural Sociology* 70(2): 188–207.

Oliker, Stacey J. 1998. "The Modernisation of Friendship: Individualism, Intimacy, and Gender in the Nineteenth Century." In *Placing Friendship in Context*, edited by Rebecca G. Adams and Graham Allan. Cambridge: Cambridge University Press.

Packard, Vance. 1972. *A Nation of Strangers*. New York: McKay.

Pedahzur, Ami, and Arie Perliger. 2006. "The Changing Nature of Suicide Attacks: A Social Network Perspective." *Social Forces* 84(4): 1987–2008.

Peplau, Letitia Anne, and Daniel Perlman. 1982. "Perspectives on Loneliness." In *Loneliness: A Sourcebook of Current Theory, Research, and Therapy,* edited by Letitia Anne Peplau and Daniel Perlman. New York: Wiley.

Pescosolido, Bernice A., Jack K. Martin, Bruce G. Link, Saeko Kikuzawa, Giovani Burgos, Ralph Swindle, and Jo Phelan. 2010. "Americans' Views of Mental Illness and Health at Century's End: Continuity and Change." Public Report on the MacArthur Mental Health Module. Bloomington: Indiana University, Department of Sociology, Indiana Consortium for Mental Health Services Research.

Pew Research Center. 2005. "Baby Boomers Approach Age 60." Available at: http://pewresearch.org/assets/social/pdf/socialtrends-boomers120805.pdf (accessed September 24, 2010).

Pollard, William E. N.d. "Use of Consumer Panel Survey Data for Public Health Communication Planning: An Evaluation of Survey Results." Atlanta: Centers for Disease Control and Prevention, Office of Communication.

Presser, Harriet. 2003. *Working in a 24/7 Economy: Challenges for American Families.* New York: Russell Sage Foundation.

———. 2004. "The Economy That Never Sleeps." *Contexts* 3(2): 42–49.

Putnam, Robert D. 2000. *Bowling Alone: The Collapse and Revival of American Community.* New York: Simon & Schuster.

———. 2007. "E Pluribus Unum: Diversity and Community in the Twenty-first Century." *Scandinavian Political Studies* 30(2): 138–75.

Quell, Carsten, Ben Veenhof, Barry Wellman, and Bernie Hogan. 2007. "Isolation, Cohesion, or Transformation? How Canadians' Use of the Internet Is Shaping Society." Paper presented to the Statistics Canada "Socio-Economic Conference." Ottawa (April 30, 2007).

Rahn, Wendy M., and John E. Transue. 1998. "Social Trust and Value Change: The Decline of Social Capital in American Youth, 1976–1995." *Political Psychology* 19(September): 545–65.

Rainie, Lee, John Horrigan, Barry Wellman, and Jeffrey Boase. 2006. "The Strength of Internet Ties." Washington, D. C.: Pew Internet and American Life Project.

Rainie, Lee, and Barry Wellmann. 2011. *Networked: The New Social Operating System.* Cambridge, Mass.: M.I.T. Press.

Ramey, Garey, and Valerie E. Ramey. 2010. "The Rug Rat Race." Unpublished paper. San Diego: University of California, Department of Economics (January).

Reinhold, Steffan. 2010. "Reassessing the Link Between Premarital Cohabitation and Marital Instability." *Demography* 47(August): 719–33.

Reschovsky, Clara. 2004. "Journey to Work: 2000." Census 2000 brief C2KBR-33. Washington: U.S. Bureau of the Census (March).

Riesman, David, in collaboration with Reuel Denney and Nathan Glazer. 1950. *The Lonely Crowd: A Study of the Changing American Character.* New Haven, Conn.: Yale University Press.

Robinson, John P., and Geoffrey Godbey. 1999. *Time for Life: The Surprising Ways Americans Use Their Time*. University Park: Pennsylvania State University Press.

Robinson, John P., and Steven Martin. 2009. "Of Time and Television." *Annals of the American Academy of Political and Social Science* 625(1): 74–86.

Robinson, Keith, and Robert F. Schoeni. 2010. "Disparities in Familial Financial Assistance to Young Adults: Initial Findings." Unpublished paper. Ann Arbor, Mich.: Institute for Social Research.

Robinson, Robert V., and Elton F. Jackson. 2001. "Is Trust in Others Declining in America? An Age-Period-Cohort Analysis." *Social Science Research* 30(1): 117–45.

Rook, Karen S. 1984. "The Negative Side of Social Interaction: Impact on Psychological Well-being." *Journal of Personality and Social Psychology* 46(5): 1097–1108.

———. 1989. "Strains in Older Adults' Friendships." In *Older Adult Friendship: Structure and Process*, edited by Rebecca G. Adams and Rosemary Blieszner. Newbury Park, Calif.: Sage Publications.

Rosenthal, Edward C. 2005. *The Era of Choice: The Ability to Choose and Its Transformation of Contemporary Life*. Cambridge, Mass.: MIT Press.

Rosenzweig, Roy, and David Thelen. 1998. *The Presence of the Past: Popular Uses of History in American Life*. New York: Columbia University Press.

Rotundo, E. Anthony. 1989. "Romantic Friendship: Male Intimacy and Middle-Class Youth in the Northern United States, 1800–1900." *Journal of Social History* 23(fall): 1–25.

Routasalo, Pirkko E., Niina Savikko, Reijo S. Tilvis, Timo E. Strandberg, and Kaisu H. Pitkälä. 2006. "Social Contacts and Their Relationship to Loneliness Among Aged People: A Population-Based Study." *Gerontology* 52(3): 181–87.

Ruan, Danching, Linton C. Freeman, Xinyuan Dai, Yunkang Pan, and Wenhong Zhang. 1997. "On the Changing Structure of Social Networks in Urban China." *Social Networks* 19(1): 75–89.

Rubenstein, Carin, and Phillip Shaver. 1982. "The Experience of Loneliness." In *Loneliness: A Sourcebook of Current Theory, Research, and Therapy*, edited by Letitia Anne Peplau and Daniel Perlman. New York: Wiley.

Russell, Daniel W. 1996. "UCLA Loneliness Scale (Version 3): Reliability, Validity, and Factor Structure." *Journal of Personality Assessment* 66(1): 20–40.

Sandberg, John F., and Sandra L. Hofferth. 2005. "Changes in Children's Time with Parents: A Correction." *Demography* 42(2): 391–95.

Sander, Thomas H., and Robert D. Putnam. 2010. "Still Bowling Alone? The Post-9/11 Split." *Journal of Democracy* 21(1): 9–16.

Schnittker, Jason. 2007. "Look Closely at All the Lonely People: Age and the Social Psychology of Social Support." *Journal of Aging and Health* 19(4): 659–82.

Schoeni, Robert F., and Karen E. Ross. 2005. "Material Assistance from Families During the Transition to Adulthood." In *On the Frontier of Adulthood: Theory, Research, and Public Policy*, edited by Richard Settersten, Frank Furstenberg, and Rubén Rumbaut. Chicago: University of Chicago Press.

Schuman, Howard. 2008. *Method and Meaning in Polls and Surveys*. Cambridge, Mass.: Harvard University Press.

Schwartz, Barry. 2004. *The Paradox of Choice: Why More Is Less*. New York: Ecco/HarperCollins.

Settersten, Richard, Frank Furstenberg, and Rubén Rumbaut, eds. 2005. *On the Frontier of Adulthood: Theory, Research, and Public Policy.* Chicago: University of Chicago Press.

Shklovski, Irina, Robert Kraut, and Lee Rainie. 2006. "The Internet and Social Participation: Contrasting Cross-Sectional and Longitudinal Analyses." *Journal of Computer-Mediated Communication* 10(1): Available at: http://online library.wiley.com/doi/10.1111/j.1083-6101.2004.tb00226.x/full (accessed September 19, 2010).

Silver, Allan. 1990. "Friendship in Commercial Society: Eighteenth-Century Social Theory and Modern Sociology." *American Journal of Sociology* 95(6): 1474–1504.

———. 1997. " 'Two Different Sorts of Commerce': Friendship and Strangership in Civil Society." In *Public and Private in Thought and Practice: Perspectives on a Grand Dichotomy,* edited by Jeff Weintraub and Krishan Kumar. Chicago: University of Chicago Press.

Silverstein, Merril, Daphna Gans, and Frances M. Yang. 2006. "Intergenerational Support to Aging Parents: The Role of Norms and Needs." *Journal of Family Issues* 27(8): 1068–84.

Silverstein, Merril, Tonya M. Parrott, and Vern L. Bengtson. 1995. "Factors That Predispose Middle-Aged Sons and Daughters to Provide Social Support to Older Parents." *Journal of Marriage and Family* 57(2): 465–75.

Smith, Christian, with Patricia Snell. 2009. *Souls in Transition: The Religious and Spiritual Lives of Emerging Adults.* New York: Oxford University Press.

Smith, Tom W. 1997. "Factors Relating to Misanthropy in Contemporary American Society." *Social Science Research* 26(June): 170–96.

———. 1998. "Why Our Neck of the Woods Is Better Than the Forest." *The Public Perspective* 9(June/July): 50–53.

Smock, Pamela J. 2000. "Cohabitation in the United States: An Appraisal of Research Themes, Findings, and Implications." *Annual Review of Sociology* 26: 1–20.

Stearns, Peter N. 1999. *Battleground of Desire: The Struggle for Self-Control in Modern America.* New York: New York University Press.

———. 2003. *Anxious Parents: A History of Modern Childrearing in America.* New York: New York University Press.

Stearns, Peter N., and Jan Lewis, eds. 1998. *An Emotional History of the United States.* New York: New York University Press.

Straits, Bruce C. 2000. "Ego's Important Discussants or Significant People: An Experiment in Varying the Wording of Personal Network Name Generators." *Social Networks* 22(2): 123–40.

Stueve, Ann, and Laura Lein. 1979. "Problems in Network Analysis: The Case of the Missing Person." Paper presented to the 32nd annual meeting of the Gerontological Society. Washington, D.C. (November).

Swaan, Abram de. 1995. "Widening Circles of Identification: Emotional Concerns in Sociogenetic Perspective." *Theory, Culture, and Society* 12(2): 25–39.

Swartz, Teresa Toguchi. 2009. "Intergenerational Family Relations in Adulthood: Patterns, Variations, and Implications in the Contemporary United States." *Annual Review of Sociology* 35: 191–212.

Swindle, Ralph, Jr., Kenneth Heller, Bernice Pescosolido, and Saeko Kikuzawa. 2000. "Responses to Nervous Breakdowns in America over a Forty-Year Period: Mental Health Policy Implications." *American Psychologist* 55(7): 740–49.

Thoits, Peggy A. 1995. "Stress, Coping, and Social Support Processes: Where Are We? What Next?" *Journal of Health and Social Behavior* (extra issue): 53–79.

Tourangeau, Roger, Lance J. Rips, and Kenneth Rasinski. 2000. *The Psychology of the Survey Response*. New York: Cambridge University Press.

Tourangeau, Roger, and Tom W. Smith. 1996. "Asking Sensitive Questions: The Impact of Data Collection Mode, Question Format, and Question Context." *Public Opinion Quarterly* 60(2): 275–304.

Trzesniewski, Kali H., and M. Brent Donnellan. Forthcoming. "Rethinking 'Generation Me': A Study of Cohort Effects from 1976 to 2006." *Perspectives in Psychological Science.*

Trzesniewski, Kali H., M. Brent Donnellan, and Richard W. Robins. 2008. "Is 'Generation Me' Really More Narcissistic Than Previous Generations?" *Journal of Personality* 76(August): 903–18.

Twenge, Jean M. 2001. "Birth Cohort Changes in Extraversion: A Cross-Temporal Meta-Analysis, 1966–1993." *Personality and Individual Differences* 30(5): 735–48.

Umberson, Debra, Robert Crosnoe, and Corinne Reczek. 2010. "Social Relationships and Health Behavior Across the Life Course." *Annual Review of Sociology* 36: 139–57.

Uslaner, Eric M. 2002. *The Moral Foundations of Trust*. New York: Cambridge University Press.

———. Forthcoming. "Does Diversity Drive Down Trust?" In *Civil Society, the State, and Social Capital: Theory, Evidence, Policy,* edited by Per Selle and Sanjeev Prakash. London: Routledge.

Utz, Rebecca L., Deborah Carr, Randolph Nesse, and Camille B. Wortman. 2002. "The Effect of Widowhood on Older Adults' Social Participation: An Evaluation of Activity, Disengagement, and Continuity Theories." *The Gerontologist* 42(4): 522–33.

van Baarsen, Berna, Marijtje A. J. van Duijn, Johannes H. Smit, Tom A. B. Snijders, and Kees C. P. M. Knipscheer. 2001–2002. "Patterns of Adjustment to Partner Loss in Old Age: The Widowhood Adaptation Longitudinal Study." *Omega* 44(1): 5–36.

van der Poel, Mart G. M. 1993a. "Personal Networks." Ph.D. diss., Katholieke Universiteit Nijmegen, Netherlands.

———. 1993b. "Delineating Personal Support Networks." *Social Networks* 15(1): 49–70.

van Groenou, Marjolein Broese, Eric van Sondoren, and Johan Ormel. 1990. "Test-Retest Reliability of Personal Network Delineation." In *Social Network Research: Substantive Issues and Methodological Questions,* edited by Kees C. P. M. Knipscheer and Toni C. Antonucci. Amsterdam: Swets & Zeitlanger.

van Sondoren, Eric, Johan Ormel, Els Brilman, and Chiquit van Linden van den Heuval. 1990. "Personal Network Delineation: A Comparison of the Exchange, Affective, and Role-Relation Approach." In *Social Network Research: Substantive Issues and Methodological Questions,* edited by Kees C. P. M. Knipscheer and Toni C. Antonucci. Amsterdam: Swets & Zeitlanger.

van Tilburg, Theo. 1998. "Interviewer Effects in the Measurement of Personal Network Size: A Non-Experimental Study." *Sociological Methods and Research* 26(3): 300–328.

Veroff, Joseph, Elizabeth Douvan, and Richard A. Kulka. 1981. *The Inner American: A Self-Portrait from 1957 to 1976.* New York: Basic Books.

Victor, Christina R., Sasha J. Scambler, Ann Bowling, and John Bond. 2005. "The Prevalence of, and Risk Factors for, Loneliness in Later Life: A Survey of Older People in Great Britain." *Ageing and Society* 25(3): 357–75.

Wang, Hua, and Barry Wellman. 2010. "Social Connectivity in America: Changes in Adult Friendship Network Size from 2002 to 2007." *American Behavioral Scientist* 53(8): 1148–70.

Watts, Duncan J. 2003. *Six Degrees: The Science of a Connected Age.* New York: Norton.

Wellman, Barry. 1979. "The Community Question." *American Journal of Sociology* 84(March): 1201–31.

———. 2004. "Connecting Communities: On and Offline." *Contexts* 3(fall): 22–28.

Witte, James. 2004. "Prologue: The Case for Multimethod Research." In *Society Online: The Internet in Context,* edited by Philip N. Howard and Steve Jones. Thousand Oaks, Calif.: Sage Publications.

Wuthnow, Robert. 1994. *Sharing the Journey: Support Groups and America's New Quest for Community.* New York: Free Press.

Index

Boldface numbers refer to figures and tables.